The *Horse Illustrated* Guide to
Advanced English Riding

By Sharon Biggs

BOWTIE
P R E S S

A Division of BowTie, Inc.
Irvine, California

Karla Austin, *Business Operations Manager*
Nick Clemente, *Special Consultant*
Barbara Kimmel, *Managing Editor*
Jessica Knott, *Production Supervisor*
Amy Stirnkorb, *Designer*
Indexed by Melody Englund

Cover photo: © Moira C. Harris
The additional photos in this book are by © CLiX Photography, pp. 10, 22, 44, 54, 60, 66, 96, 123, 140, 144, 149, 150, 158, 160, 162, 168, 172, 175, 176, 181; © Moira C. Harris, 12, 14, 15, 17, 18, 19, 20, 21, 23, 24, 28, 31, 32, 33, 34, 38, 41, 45, 47, 48, 51, 53, 56, 57, 59, 61, 62, 63, 64, 68, 69, 71, 74, 76, 77, 78, 80, 82, 84, 86, 88, 89, 90, 92, 93, 95, 98, 100, 101, 102, 121, 125, 126, 128, 132, 133, 134, 136, 137, 138, 152, 153, 154, 156, 170, 171, 179; © Amber Heintzberger, 8, 27, 104, 106, 107, 109, 111, 113, 114, 115, 116, 142,145, 164, 166, 178; © Lesley Ward, 30, 36, 118, 120, 124, 130, 147, 182, 188, 196

The horses in this book are referred to as *she* and *he* in alternating chapters unless their sexes are apparent from the activity discussed.

Library of Congress Cataloging-in-Publication Data

Library of Congress Cataloging-in-Publication Data

Biggs, Sharon, 1966–
   The horse illustrated guide to advanced English riding / by Sharon Biggs.
      p. cm.
   Includes bibliographical references and index.
   ISBN 978-1-931993-88-3
   1. Horsemanship. I. Title.

   SF309.B54 2007
   798.2'3—dc22
                                        2007000320

BowTie Press®
A Division of BowTie, Inc.
3 Burroughs
Irvine, California 92618

Printed and bound in Singapore
16 15 14 13 12 11 10 09 08 07   1 2 3 4 5 6 7 8 9 10

Dedication

For my parents, who encouraged me to become a rider and a writer; and for Mark, my lifelong riding partner.

Contents

Contents

Contents

Acknowledgments

No rider can make it through his or her career without being influenced by others, and an equestrian journalist is no different. I drew inspiration and gained expertise for this project, directly and indirectly, from several fine riders, including Sidley Paine, Christopher Bartle, Mark Waller, Richard Spooner, Kass Lockhart, Maryne Langer, Amber Heintzberger, Cindy Hale, Jane Weatherwax, Perry Wood, Richard Davidson, Karen Dixon, Mike Winter, Blyth Tate, and Timmie Pollock. Special thanks to models Laura Forrester, Katie and Joe Lifto, Lori Gabrelli, and Sherie Grant.

I also owe a debt of gratitude to Moira Harris, a wonderful editor, photographer, and good friend who encouraged me throughout this project.

Introduction

What is the definition of an advanced rider? More than at any other level, the advanced rider possesses a broad spectrum of skills at various stages of development. There are many levels of advancement. Of course, someone who has reached the dizzying heights of Olympic competition is an advanced rider, but a person who has learned the fundamentals of riding and gone on to own a horse of his or her own also can be an advanced rider. For me, the beginning advanced rider is someone who grasps the idea of good horsemanship and puts a great deal of time and effort into developing his or her seat and position. This book will help you develop those skills, and it is my hope that it will also help give you the skills to move on to the next step of your riding career, whatever the final level may be.

Honing the Seat and Position

All advanced riders want to achieve an independent position. Independence means that you're in total control of your seat at all times, no matter what your horse does—even if she spooks or bucks. This seat allows you to move with any horse's stride and with your legs lightly against your horse's barrel, instead of gripping for balance. An independent seat also means you have the ability to maintain a steady contact with your reins, instead of using them as a way to stay on. Most of all, an independent position means you can time your aids correctly and use them effectively.

Checking Your Seat

To sit well, the rider has to be in a vertical line, over his own feet. Think about the best position to take if you are standing on the ground. You won't stand with your upper body pitched forward or back; you'll stand with your knees slightly bent, and your hips will be over your feet so your feet, your hips, and your shoulders are aligned vertically. In the saddle, you want the middle of your foot (in the stirrup) to be underneath your hip, with your knee bent to whatever degree your kind of riding dictates. Your shoulders should be in line with your hips and your feet. You also must be balanced laterally, side to side, and have equal weight in the stirrups, with your shoulders parallel to the horse's shoulders and your hips parallel to the horse's hips.

Here is an example of a good dressage position: shoulders, hips, and feet aligned, with shoulders parallel to the horse's shoulders and hips parallel to the horse's hips.

As you put your leg on the horse and ask for driving energy from the hind legs, the energy must be able to travel through your seat, which says to the horse, "I want you to stay in this length of stride, in this tempo, and in this gait." Then your hand has to receive and direct that energy. Riders often want to know how much leg pressure they should use. Remember that a horse can feel a fly on his coat, so your aids don't have to be huge to get a response; however, they have to mean something, or your horse will ignore you, and deservedly so. Therefore, whenever you use your legs, make sure that what you are asking for is clear and that you receive the correct response. Don't wait five seconds or more. Repeat the request. Your horse may require a tap from the whip, paired with the leg pressure, until she understands that you mean what you say. Spurs are also a good aid, but make sure your leg position is rock solid before you use them. Spurs used incorrectly can make your horse dull to or, worse, frightened of your leg. The rule of thumb regarding leg pressure is to use just enough to squash a ripe tomato against your horse's side. And always keep your legs against your horse, close enough to feel her coat against your boots. Hold your legs there at all times, even when posting, because bouncing legs can cause your horse to become dull to your aids.

Good Hands

Although the different styles of English riding require a variety of hand positions, the overall purpose of the hands remains the same: to communicate your intentions to the horse (for example, slow down, turn here, stop). Your hands are, in effect, a telephone and a way to relay your requests. These requests must be clear and easily understood. If not, your horse will be confused and frustrated and will give you the wrong response or ignore you altogether. Tense, unfeeling, or jostling hands create an uncomfortable pressure that even the kindest horse will come to resent. Riders with light, open hands that barely touch the reins arc just as at fault; although not as uncomfortable for the horse, lack of contact is tantamount to lack of conversation.

For dressage riders, a good hand position is about more than just hands. The position includes the use of the whole arm: elbow, forearm, and shoulder. The arm must be in an L shape, with the elbow bent. If you hand a rider a stack of books and she lifts only her forearm from the elbow and takes the books, she can hold that L-shaped position for a long time. If she extends that arm out from her body, even four inches, she won't be able to hold those books for very long because her arms will pull her shoulders forward, and she will be unbalanced.

13

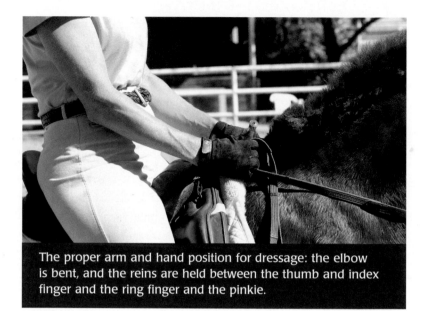

The proper arm and hand position for dressage: the elbow is bent, and the reins are held between the thumb and index finger and the ring finger and the pinkie.

To avoid holding with tension, imagine that your hands are an extension of your elbows. Riding from the elbow forward will keep you from gripping the rein. If you have to get demanding in your conversation (let's say, for instance, your horse is getting strong and trying to pull the reins away), you can tighten your elbows and prevent her from running through your hands. Even with firm elbows, you'll still be able to keep those quiet, soft hands.

The dressage rein is held between the thumb and the first and second knuckles of the index finger and passes between the ring finger and the pinkie (held between the first and second knuckles of the ring finger). The thumb creates enough pressure to keep the reins from sliding loose, and each finger stacks evenly on top of the next. In this manner, your sense of touch is much more sensitive than if your reins are held toward the backs of your fingers.

The use of this hand position is very simple. Squeeze your right ring finger against the rein if you want your horse to flex right, and squeeze your left ring finger if you want your horse to flex left.

Squeeze one or both reins for a half halt. If you need a stronger aid, say for a sharper turn, think of turning a doorknob. If you want to go right, gently turn your right fist as though you are turning a doorknob to the right. Note: If your horse isn't responding, check that your reins are the proper lengths. The reins should be short enough to enable you to feel your horse's mouth.

For hunter and jumper riders, the elbows are held in front of the body. This is because the body position for hunter equitation and jumping has to be more forward. In dressage, with the more upright position, you have the weight of your body to help when using the reins, which gives you more leverage. In jumping, you need a shorter length of rein to achieve the same sort of leverage. Hands should be held an inch apart and an inch above the horse's crest.

Fingers should be curled inward and closed against the hand in a relaxed manner, and all your fingers should face one another. This position allows the bit to work flush against the horse's cheek. When your hands are flat and wide, the bit gets pulled away from the horse's face and does not work as well. Turning your hands down also puts a dead weight on the reins and into the horse's mouth, encouraging her to lean.

For huntseat, the rider's elbows are slightly forward and the fingers are curled inward and closed against the hand.

For this hand position, think of using your rein as if your arm were a door: your hand is the knob, your forearm is the door, and the space between your hip and your elbow is the hinge. Your arm and hand (with a straight wrist) together swing around your entire body, moving toward the horse's hip. This gives you a greater range of motion because you can move your hand from the withers all the way around your body. If you just use your wrist, you have only one or two inches of movement. This is fine in dressage, but when you are jumping a course, you need the ability to make short direction changes faster.

For all disciplines, to keep a soft contact on your horse's mouth, your hand and arm positions must follow the movement of the horse's head and neck in each gait. At the walk, your elbows move back as your hips move forward and out as your hips move back. At the trot, the positions remain steady. At the canter and gallop, they move forward and back, along with the motion of your seat.

Riding the Gaits

You may have noticed while lunging your horse that her movements affect the saddle in different ways: the trot makes the saddle move up and down, the canter moves it in a twisting motion, and the walk moves it forward and back. Very simply put, to ride the gaits properly, you must follow these motions with your seat.

The Sitting Trot

In the sitting trot, some horses are very smooth, and their riders don't have to do much more than sit. Other horses are very bouncy; many riders respond by trying to sit as still as possible, but this never works. The horse is moving so you must move with her. When the horse is in her suspension phase, the sitting trot feels as though you are catapulted up, to a greater or lesser degree depending on the horse; when she comes down from the suspension, you fall back into the saddle. If you are sitting the trot correctly, you learn to absorb that up-and-down movement in your knees, in your hips, and slightly in your ankles. If you brace your leg out in front of you, no shock will be absorbed.

Sit so that your upper body is disturbed as little as possible. Because your upper body is high above the horse, you influence her balance. If your shoulders are flopping from side to side, you may cause her to stagger sideways, which may force her to throw her head up into the air for balance. This is where your core muscles come in. If you flex your back muscles and stomach muscles, you will hold your seat to the saddle.

Try this exercise. While riding in an enclosed space, pick up the sitting trot, and hold the pommel with your outside hand and the cantle with your inside hand (this turns your body in the direction

This is a good position for the sitting trot.

Here a strap of leather has been laced through the D rings of the saddle's pommel to create a "cheater" strap.

the horse is moving). Alternatively, you can lace a leather strap or the bottom half of an old drop noseband through the D rings of your pommel to create a "cheater" strap. If your horse is calm, tie the reins in a knot, hold them against the pommel, and let your horse follow the arena wall around. It is very important that you don't grip with your butt, thighs, or calves. If you grip, you are going to bounce because you will be holding yourself down with the wrong muscles. You must use your upper body to press your seat into the saddle. This means keeping your stomach and back relatively still, without tilting forward and back on the pelvis as people often do. Don't wiggle your stomach, and don't arch your back and stick your bottom out behind you. Ideally, exert a steady, constant pressure on your seat bones. This technique takes a long time to develop. As you get better, loosen your grip on the strap to teach your back to stay with the saddle. If your horse is trained to go in side reins, you can also repeat this exercise on the lunge.

Bouncing is a common theme in the early stages of the sitting trot; the important thing to know is that when you bounce up you'll fall back down into the same place. You can catch yourself with your knees if you happen to fall sideways, but then relax your knees again so your sitting bones can fall on the saddle. If the horse's back is properly relaxed and her neck is down, you won't hurt her. A horse will object, however, if the rider pulls on the reins as she bounces.

Another reason people bounce is that their shoulders are stiff. Learn to relax your shoulders with this exercise. Holding the pommel with your outside hand, swing your inside arm up and back in rhythmic circles, calmly and with a soft shoulder, in time with the horse's movement. Switch arms, and when you are comfortable, circle both arms at the same time, grabbing the pommel when necessary. A variation on this exercise is the shoulder shrug: lightly holding the pommel with both hands, shrug your shoulders up, back, and around in circles.

While riding on the lunge, learn to relax your shoulders with arm circles, as demonstrated.

For a good back-strengthening exercise, hold your arm up and stretch it back while riding a sitting trot, as shown.

To strengthen your back, pick up the sitting trot, hold one arm up straight, and stretch it back to tighten the back muscles.

By this time, you should be able to pick up the reins; however, check to be sure you are ready. Put your hands in the rein-holding position with no reins, and see if your hands jump up and down. If they do, you need to relax your elbows and shoulders. You can also learn to stabilize your hand by resting the bottom part of the hand on the pommel as you sit the trot. (Note: the hunter rider sits in a similar dressage position while sitting the trot, rather than leaning forward in a two-point position.)

The Posting Trot

The posting trot is an important skill to perfect, particularly since we use it so much of the time. An improved posting trot will give you steadier hands, better control of your leg aids, and a softer seat.

A hunter or jumper rider should lean forward and post forward and backward. In the posting trot, the rider's shoulders should be inclined slightly forward, about 30 degrees from vertical. At this angle, you can move with the horse's motion, which in turn allows your horse to trot out better. Hunter and jumper riders also use the posting trot as a tool to get off the horse's back and allow her to stretch her neck out and forward.

A dressage rider, on the other hand, should sit over the vertical with shoulders and hips aligned. The thighs should hang as straight as possible; the knees should be slightly bent. The shoulders should never lean forward. The hips should rise out of the saddle and forward over the pommel and land back in the saddle in the same place. In this position, the rider is able to keep her lower leg quietly against the horse's barrel throughout the phase of the posting trot so she can use it when needed. This position also helps the horse arch her frame and encourage her haunches under.

The hunter/jumper rider posts the trot with the slightly forward body angle shown here, about 30 degrees from the vertical.

The dressage rider posts the trot by rising and sitting over the vertical as shown, with shoulders and hips aligned.

The Canter

To ride the canter, let's look at lunging once more. Think about the motion of the saddle as your horse canters. It moves in a twisting fashion. Your seat must move in a similar twisting way in balance with your horse. Some instructors may urge you to ride the canter with a forward-and-back motion, the way a child rides a rocking horse. This is a good visual for the beginning stages of your riding career, but you'll need to add another piece of the puzzle at this stage of your skills. The horse's leading leg will cause the twist to be canted more to one side than the other. Therefore, your inside hip should twist farther forward than your outside hip. Hold your shoulders still and allow your lower back to be soft and move with your horse.

The Hand Gallop and the Gallop

Hand gallop means the horse is still "in hand," or controllable. Lengthening the stride and slightly increasing the speed is your goal. The hand gallop is used in lower levels of eventing; the speed at

In the canter, the rider's inside hip twists a bit farther forward than her outside hip, with still shoulders and a soft lower back, as demonstrated here.

Novice is set at canter speed, 375 mpm (meters per minute, the universal unit of measurement for gait speed), increasing to 450 mpm at Training. Jumpers compete above 375 mpm, so this gait is used frequently in competition. The hand gallop also can be used as a schooling exercise for dressage horses to produce a more forward and expressive canter.

The hand gallop and gallop positions are very similar to the jumping, or two-point, position. In this position, you no longer sit in the saddle. You take the seat, your third point of contact, away and ride from the heel up to the knee. Looking up and straight ahead will make you a much softer, much more forward rider. The most important concerns are that your hands are low, that the foundation of the position is in your lower leg, and that you're not using the horse's mouth for balance.

Hold the reins in the usual way in the hand gallop. In the gallop, hold your reins in either the half bridge or the full bridge. For the half bridge, stretch one rein across the horse's neck so that you're

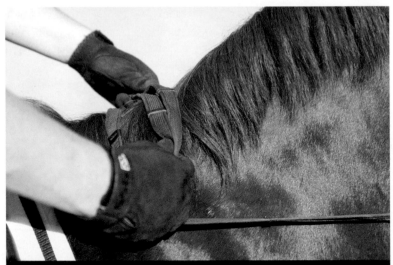

This is the correct hand position for the full bridge used in a gallop.

This is the correct hand position for the half bridge used in a gallop.

holding two pieces of leather in one hand. For the full bridge, stretch both reins across the horse's neck so that both hands are holding two pieces of leather. The reins will be pulled across the horse's crest instead of hanging in a loop alongside the neck. The bridges are also very useful tools in terms of safety. If your horse were to stumble, the bridge can keep you from falling because your arms won't collapse on either side of the horse's neck.

The gallop is the gait at which event riders shine. In fact, most cross-country work is performed at the gallop. Preliminary eventing speed is set at 520 mpm, Intermediate speed at 550 mpm, and Advanced speed at 570 mpm. Knowing how to ride at a specific eventing speed is an important skill. To learn what each speed feels like, set up a meters-per-minute track. You will need a measuring wheel (available at tack stores, hardware stores, or home improvement centers); stakes with flags; and a long, even stretch of ground with decent footing. Measure out the distance on the gallops, and place a stake in the ground for whatever speed you want to learn: 375 meters out from the start of your gallop for the canter; 400 to 450 meters for the hand gallop; 520, 550, and 570 meters for the upper levels. Wear a watch and time yourself from the starting point. You should reach your chosen stake in one minute.

The best way to gallop is to begin slowly and build up to it gradually. This is advisable because some horses get high on the speed, and a fast start can undo the hard work you've put into training an obedient horse that listens to your aids. When you're eventing, leave the start box at a trot, then go into a canter, then a hand gallop, and then the gallop to ensure that your horse is still listening and rideable.

When jumper riders gallop in a class against time, they treat the gallop much the same as the hand gallop, a little bit quicker but not so fast that they knock the fence down. To practice, gallop toward the fence, and then slow down or "balance up" a few strides in front of the fence to allow your horse to get her legs underneath her to jump.

Galloping requires a lot from a horse, and she can injure herself badly if her body isn't used to concussion at top speed. Think long and hard about whether galloping is right for you and your horse. The once-a-week rider should not gallop: galloping is for people who ride their horses five times a week. If you think galloping is for you, you must work up to it by conditioning your horse. Most event riders gallop once every five days, but your horse may not be up to this schedule. Warm up with ten to twenty minutes of trotting, then begin with three minutes at the hand gallop, two minutes at a walk, and another three minutes at the hand gallop. Then, after a few weeks or months (consult a trainer if you are unsure how to test your horse's fitness level), progressively increase the gallop speed to 450 mpm for three minutes, followed by the two-minute walk and then the second gallop at 500 mpm for three minutes. This interval training builds your horse's cardiovascular system and soft tissue.

You should also outfit your horse in the appropriate bit for galloping, one that gives you adequate control. For some horses, this might be a simple snaffle; for others, it might be something stronger. A flash or figure-eight noseband is important because it ensures the horse will keep her mouth closed, which will also help you maintain control. If the horse's mouth is open, no bit will work. Your horse should also be wearing brushing boots for protection. Polo wraps can come undone or slip, and a horse can trip or fall if she steps on a loose wrap.

Refrain from galloping in wooded areas. It's hard to gauge your speed and see what's ahead or coming at you in the other direction. Before you gallop, walk the area to check for holes and debris and to make sure the ground is not too hard, deep, or slippery. Understand that your speed (when you're practicing) will depend on what the land and conditions allow. You can turn only so sharply or go downhill safely at only certain speeds. As you go faster, the balance of the horse should always stay the same.

This horse is properly equipped for galloping, with a flash
noseband on the bridle and brushing boots on the legs.

2

The Half Halt

The half halt is probably one of the most misunderstood skills in riding. Many riders find it difficult because they focus too much on the physical mechanics of the aid. Concentrating on thinking it through makes the aid last too long, and the rider ends up mistiming the half halt or pulling against the horse. The half halt is actually momentary. It shouldn't last longer than one footfall of the horse.

The name of the skill is a great description of what it does: it halfway halts the horse. To analyze it a step further, the half halt works by slowing the front end momentarily. Because you are still asking the horse to move forward, the hind legs continue to do so; as a result, the horse's frame briefly becomes more compact, and he begins to move with his topline arched. This posture helps the horse balance on his haunches rather than on his forehand or, worse, on your hands. And from this posture, he will be able to carry out the changes that you are about to ask for, such as a turn, a transition, or a change in tempo (speed). You'll feel that the horse is easier to influence and more comfortable to ride. You'll also feel a sense of being with the horse rather than somewhere behind him. The horse's movement will be more fluid. The flow of energy between the two of you will also become more fluid. It will feel easier to sit to the trot and the canter. The horse will also feel stronger and taller and arched in his back.

Besides slowing and balancing the horse, the half halt has other benefits. Horses tend to take over the tempo and the center of balance to make things easier for themselves. Typically, you're riding

The use of the half halt will help keep your horse balanced in the canter, like this.

around thinking all is well until you try to circle. Suddenly, you realize your horse is off in a world of his own. The half halt reminds him to be a team player and to listen to your communication. It's often a little reminder that you're the one who's setting the agenda.

The Anatomy of the Half Halt

Here is a breakdown of the important elements of the half halt:

- Make sure that as you ride along your back is flowing with the movement of the horse. If you always sit stiffly against him, he won't be able to feel the half halt coming through your seat.
- Lengthen your legs slightly so that the lower leg asks the horse to step a little deeper with his hind legs.
- Decrease the flow of your back and seat by gently firming the muscles along your spine for a split second. Your horse may feel this resistance and think, "Oh, she wants to stop," and begin to shift his balance back in anticipation of the halt.

Half halts need to be customized to suit each horse. This horse is resisting the rider's request to halt.

The rider makes the half halt more emphatic, and the horse responds.

- If your elbow is hanging directly under your shoulder and not in front or pulled too far behind, the resistance from your spine will move down your arm and into the rein. Don't pull the reins. If you need to get your point across to your horse, squeeze the reins rather than pull back.
- Your *lower* leg should remain lightly on the horse throughout and ready to send him forward again. As you feel the horse make the shift down, apply your leg aid, soften your spine, and move forward again.

The rider responds to the horse by softening the contact. The horse has halted well.

Here the rider applies the half halt just when the horse's outside foreleg is forward.

The most effective moment to apply the half halt is when the outside foreleg is going forward. That makes the outside foreleg take a slightly shorter step.

The Wrong Ways to Half Halt

Riders commonly make the following mistakes when using the half halt:

Making the half halt last too long. Riders often eliminate the middleman of softening the spine by continuing to brace against the horse and continuing to pull on the rein. They wait for the horse to give before they give. The half halt must last no longer than a stride, whether it works or not. If it hasn't worked, repeat it slightly more emphatically in another stride. If you hold too long, your horse will begin to fight you by leaning on your hands, rushing off, or resisting your aids. At best, the half halt lasts no longer than one stride. If it doesn't work, stop asking, then repeat it.

Focusing too much on the reins. Many riders wrongly equate the half halt with pulling on the reins. The old tug-and-release method to slow down is a crude approach to riding. However, if you feel that your horse is barging through your hand rather than pulling on the reins, reconfirm the contact by closing your fingers within your hand, much like wringing water out of a sponge. Think of riding the horse forward into an already halted bit, rather than bringing the bit backward to halt the horse.

Not thinking ahead. Riders have to act before things get out of hand. Sometimes it's too late to do a half halt: the rider has waited until the horse is really on his forehand and moving too fast. Then the momentum is so great the rider would need a half halt strong enough to stop a bus. Some horses need a half halt even in the first stride of the canter or the trot. If you ask for the half halt right away, you set the balance for the new gait so it doesn't get out of control. If you've lost control completely, halt the horse and start the transition again.

Performing the half halt mechanically. Many riders apply the half halt too technically, which means it's clumsy and it takes too long. Horses are "push into pressure" creatures, meaning that if you put pressure on the horse without knowing and communicating its

A rider avoids overthinking the half halt by paying attention to how the horse feels.

purpose, then the horse is going to resist you. The aids are mean-ingless unless they are supporting a clear idea. Riders often get wrapped up in the physical mechanics of the aid without having a concept of what the horse should feel like after they apply the aid. Try not to become obsessed with how exactly you're supposed to do it. Focus on how the horse is feeling to you. If you can't get it, ask a knowledgeable friend or instructor for help.

Forgetting to customize the half halt. Riders must keep in mind that every horse is different. They may think that they are doing the half halt correctly, but it may not be effective for that particular horse on that particular day—or in a particular situation or even at that moment. Sometimes the half halt has to be incredibly subtle to avoid ruining the (particular) flow. Sometimes it has to be repeated in a more emphatic way until you get a response.

The half halt is principally the same no matter what style of rider you are. Although hunter and jumper riders don't sit the same way as a dressage rider does, the theory is still the same. The legs engage, and a split-second resistance through the rider's body is car-ried into the reins. The horse still feels the momentary lack of flow through his rider.

Riding Within the Gaits

Riding in the beginning stages is all about the working walk, the trot, and the canter, but as you advance in your skills, everything becomes more complex. For instance, you must learn how to move seamlessly from one gait to another. You need to include paces in your repertoire; for instance, the walk paces include the free walk, the medium walk, the extended walk, and the collected walk. While jumping, you must learn to adjust your stride within the speed of your canter, hand gallop, or gallop, depending on the style of fence. Advanced riders also need to learn how to advance a horse's knowledge with a method of training. In dressage, this is primarily the training pyramid or scale. Because this is a universal, integral concept among riders of all disciplines, I urge you to incorporate this technique into your own training sessions.

Transitions

A well-ridden transition seems a simple thing. After all, in essence you are only switching gears: walk to trot, trot to canter, or trot to walk. But many things that appear easy are in actuality very hard to do. What people see in that easy transition is a horse that smoothly changes rhythm; for example, from a one-two, one-two beat in the trot to a one-two-three beat in the canter. Nothing else changes: the horse should continue to move forward with the same energy (unless you've halted), remain on the bit or accepting the bit, and stay balanced. But what brings about the shift in gaits is indiscernible to observers. That's the rider's job, to make his aids invisible to spectators and obvious only to the horse—to make the whole thing look easy. A great transition is one that is prepared and well trained, but most of all one that shows the true harmony and partnership between horse and rider that has developed over time.

If you're a dressage rider, bad transitions will keep you stuck in Training Level because the further you advance in the levels, the more important transitions become. If you're a hunter or jumper rider and you can't pull off a transition on the flat, you'll be in trouble when it comes to jumping because you won't be able to gauge your distances. You'll come into the fence too deeply or chip in an extra stride. Your hunter won't make the proper strides between fences, and your jumper will most likely pull rails.

A common fault in the downward transition is that the rider leans back and braces against the horse and uses his stirrups as brake pedals. Or he leans forward and lightens his seat. Because there is no preparation, the result is an awkward transition, or the horse either braces back and ignores the rider completely or responds by going faster. When riders brace and fall to the back of the saddle, their seat drives the horse on and makes her go faster. Everyone instinctively leans back to stop, and that's good if you're a beginning rider and you're going to fall off, but not at this stage in your riding. The answer is to keep your position through your transition.

Using the bit for a brake is another common fault. If this is your issue, go back and review your half halt and make sure you are applying it correctly.

Making an upward transition by chasing the horse until she reaches the required gait is also a common error. For example, instead of simply moving from the trot to the canter, riders gun the horse forward from the walk to a fast trot and then to the canter. In this error, the rider's seat has shifted too far forward, and he has not

This balanced rider has her horse moving in a controlled canter, ready for a smooth downward transition.

started with his horse balanced and accepting the bit. In the upward transition, keep the energy flowing from behind. Ask when your position is correct, and don't ask for the canter if your horse begins to run. Bring her back and try again, this time with better preparation. You may have also used too sharp an aid to jolt your horse forward. Ask with a softer cue.

If your horse doesn't respond to the upward transition, chances are she's ignoring your aids. Instead of beating a tattoo against your horse's ribcage, reschool her to a light leg aid. Bring your horse back to the walk, and ask her to trot on. If she won't go, pair your leg aid with a touch of your whip. If she trots on, pet her and bring her back to a walk. Then ask again with a lighter aid, turning up the volume with your whip until you can put your leg on lightly and she will trot off.

A rule of thumb for hunter and jumper/riders: If your horse is rushing and dragging you to the jump, go back and work on your transitions from the canter to the trot. If your horse is too slow and you feel that you keep getting left behind at the jump, make sure your canter departure from the walk is correct.

The Training Pyramid, or Scale

The training pyramid (also called training scale) is an important concept in dressage training. Failure to understand the dressage pyramid when training or not taking each step into account is a very common rider error. The dressage pyramid is a logical training method: each new step builds on the previous step. It begins with rhythm, followed by looseness, contact, straightness, and impulsion and ends with collection. Skip one criterion, and you won't be heading up the scale and will have difficulty advancing.

Rhythm: A pattern of steps or strides for each gait, such as the one-two-three in the canter and the one-two, one-two in the trot. The beat should be regular, and each pattern should cover equal ground. To achieve a good rhythm, your horse must be free from any soundness issues and must be able to carry the rider while staying balanced.

Looseness: Physically and mentally free from tension. The horse accepts the rider's aids and moves forward correctly at the tempo (speed) that the rider requests.

Contact: The horse moves forward toward the bit without apprehension or fear of the rider's hands. (See chapter 4, Putting Your Horse on the Bit.)

Straightness: The forehand is in line with the hindquarters, and the horse's weight is evenly distributed on both sides. If your horse is not straight, you will have trouble turning, making circles, and doing lateral work. You can feel the straightness in the ease of accomplishing all of the above.

Impulsion: Thrust or pushing power of the hind legs in the trot and the canter (the walk has no impulsion because it has no moment of suspension). The horse pushes herself through the arena instead of pulling with her front legs. With impulsion, you feel the horse taking a bigger step as you apply your legs. The gait feels stronger and more purposeful.

Collection: Increased bend of the hind legs, with the horse carrying more weight on the haunches and less on the forehand. The horse's movements are easier to ride. (See the following section.)

Collection

When a horse is collected, she brings her hind legs farther underneath her body and carries more weight in her haunches. The working gait does not require the horse to do this. The working gait also lacks a certain amount of impulsion and engagement of the hind legs. Riders often mistake collection with riding very slowly, but in truth the tempo alters very little. The horse's neck must not get shorter; in fact, it won't change in length through the dressage levels. Instead, the horse's outline will be more uphill because her front end will rise as she takes more weight back onto her haunches. Some of the hallmarks of collection are the ability to ride movements with ease and smooth and steady transitions.

This upper-level dressage horse performs the piaffe, one of the highest demonstrations of collection.

At the early levels of collection, there is only a slight difference between working and collected gaits. The collected trot you see at the lower levels is a different collected trot from that seen at Grand Prix because the horse is stronger at the higher levels. At the higher levels, collection is highlighted in advanced movements such as piaffe and passage. At the lower levels, it is demonstrated in movements such as shoulder-in and the extended gaits.

Strengthening exercises are helpful for collection. Ten-meter circles engage the inside hind leg and develop the muscles. Transitions work to develop the all-important impulsion or thrust from the hindquarters required for collection. Too much work in collection can be tiring, so keep your workout appropriate to your horse's level of training. And always end your sessions with a stretching circle.

Ride a ten-meter circle to engage the inside hind leg and develop the muscles of the hindquarters, as shown.

Extensions

Many riders are confused about what constitutes an extension. An over-stride in the medium and extended walk is a requirement in the dressage tests, but how much overstride is inconsequential; judges take into account the horse's breed, confirmation, and ability. Clarity of the rhythm, elasticity to the walk, and whether a horse moves over his topline are more important. In the trot, the horse ideally should step over the prints of his front hooves. In the canter, the horse must cover more ground.

The Extended Walk

Pay special attention to the walk because it is the easiest gait to ruin and the most difficult to correct. The extended walk paces include the free walk, the medium walk, and the extended walk. In the free walk, the horse is allowed to lower and stretch the head and neck on a loose or free rein. The medium walk should have an overstride, and the horse should stretch to and remain on the bit. In the extended walk, the horse covers more ground and stretches the head and neck out while still maintaining contact. All the walk paces should march forward with good energy and have a purity of rhythm.

In dressage competition, the walk is valuable. For instance, there are fifty points related to the walk in many of the Training and First Level tests, which incorporate the medium walk, the free walk, and the gaits scores. The free walk score is doubled. The points for the walk are high because the gait is an indicator of the quality and progress of training. A walk that becomes impure in any way or is a little uneven because of crookedness or resistance can hurt the submission score as well.

It's not just the quality of the walk that matters but also the way it's ridden. Riders often impede the horse by failing to allow her to oscillate and move her whole body. The hands are too still, trying to keep the horse on the bit. And in the free walk, riders often don't allow the horse to stretch as far as she wants to. They spend too much time worrying that she will jig or break into the trot.

This is a good example of free walk on a long rein.

You can practice the various phases of the walk at home by teaching the horse to march across the diagonal of the arena or the pattern in your dressage test. Keep the horse moving forward, in front of your leg. Never become complacent and let your horse become lazy, even when warming up or finishing your schooling session.

The Extended Trot and Canter

There are three different paces of the extended trot and canter: lengthening (encountered at First Level), medium (beginning at Second Level), and extended (found at Third Level and up). Each pace builds on the next as the horse begins to bring her balance uphill. The more collection and strength a horse builds, the bigger your extension will be, depending on your horse's ability.

A dressage horse and rider perform an extended trot.

Lengthening is developed from a working gait. Lengthenings are the precursors to extensions, but lengthenings are often mistaken for changes of speed rather than length of stride. When you lengthen a gait, the horse's frame should lengthen as well. The medium trot builds from a collected gait. When you ask for medium, you'll get more impulsion from the hind legs and a bigger stride. The extended trot is a bigger medium trot with a larger reach of the front end and stretch of the topline. A horse that brings the front legs high in front in a park-horse motion is not displaying the extension required in dressage.

It seems counterintuitive, but you won't achieve better extensions by practicing extensions. Instead, work toward extensions by developing your horse's strength through transitions. Increased strength gives you pushing power, which is what produces the longer stride. All transitions are worthy: within the gaits, from one gait to another, to the halt, and from the halt. You can then ask for your desired extension for a few steps and then come back to your collected or working gait. Shoulder-in (see chapter 6, Lateral Work) is a good advanced exercise for the medium and the extended trot. Ride a few steps of shoulder-in, then ask for a few steps of the medium or the extended gait. When schooling extensions, it is imperative that the horse stays balanced and that the rhythm and tempo remain the same. If you feel your horse faltering, bring her back, reestablish, then ask again.

Adjusting the Stride

Event riders must be able to adjust their canter, hand gallop, and gallop to three different stride lengths to be successful and, most important, safe while riding a cross-country course. Jumper riders need this skill for the odd strides often required in show jumping courses.

The three lengths include a regular stride, a short stride, and a long stride. The long stride is needed for jumps that require big strides such as ditches or water jumps. The short stride is needed for jumps that require careful riding such as the downhill approach to a bounce with vertical rails or a shortened stride in a combination. A regular stride is needed for jumps that can be taken out of the normal stride such as logs, brush jumps, or verticals.

To learn the three stride types, begin at the canter. Set two poles on the ground. For the regular stride, set them eight strides (twelve feet equals one average canter stride) apart, and count your strides as you canter from pole to pole. Canter over the first pole and say "jump," then count each following stride aloud and say "jump" as you go over the second pole. If you can count eight strides, you will have ridden regular canter strides.

To produce the more forward long canter, start with a regular canter stride. As you approach the pole, release with your elbows, put your hands forward, close your legs, and allow your horse to go in a bigger canter. You should be able to ride seven strides between the poles.

For the short stride, approach again in a regular canter, but before you approach the pole, apply a half halt to shorten the stride. You should be able to ride nine strides between the poles. With practice, you will be able to feel how much half halt you will need to shorten.

As you progress, you can increase or decrease your strides further. Challenge yourself. Instead of nine shortened strides, ask for ten. Instead of seven long strides, try for six. Once you learn this skill at the canter, you will also be able to apply it to the hand gallop and the gallop.

Flying Changes

If flying changes are not taught properly or are rushed, or if the horse is pushed, you can set back your horse's training significantly. Your horse must have solid basics before you move forward with a flying change. She must understand a half halt; complete downward and upward transitions without anticipating or objecting; and have a balanced, controlled, straight canter. If you have reached this point, then the next step is teaching your horse a simple change, which means the horse will change through either the walk or the trot. Your horse must "nail" these changes in every way. She must grasp the concept of new bend equals new lead. You can practice your simple changes through a figure eight, breaking it down to the very foundation. As you complete each circle or loop of the figure eight and approach the center, bring your horse down to a calm, straight walk for a few strides. Then look toward the new direction, bend your horse slightly, and use your new outside leg behind the girth. This will ensure a crisp canter depart onto the next lead.

Next, slowly but surely, ask for a lead change by making a simple half turn while cantering around your entire arena. For instance,

You can learn to adjust the canter stride with the aid of ground poles, as demonstrated.

while cantering on the left lead, canter down the long side and ride into the corner. Give yourself plenty of time to reverse on a twenty-meter half circle, making a diagonal line back to the long side toward the next corner. About the time you rejoin the long side, you should be at the corner. This gives your horse a visual cue that the arena rail is bending right. As you join the rail, half halt your horse so she's aware you're about to ask for a transition, then look right, bend right, and ask for your flying lead change as your horse is in the suspension phase of the canter. One tip is to put a pole on the ground to encourage the moment of suspension; this is also a good visual cue for you.

Do not shove or spur. Use the same aids you use in the simple changes. The only difference is that as you make your half halt you won't be changing gaits. If your horse gives you even half of a change, reward her. If you are frustrated and resort to using harsh aids, you will create a monster, and your horse will learn to hate her lead changes. Some horses are more talented at lead changes than others and learn faster. Some take a long time.

The breakdown for the flying change is: half halt, slight new bend with your new inside hand to the new direction. At about the same time, apply your new outside leg behind the girth as the driving aid. In dressage, you will also change your seat bone.

Changing the lead in the air is more a jumper aspect than a hunter aspect because it saves time when riding against the clock. The danger for hunters in doing a lead change in the air is that it sometimes produces a contortion in the rider's position, because you shift your weight as you ask the horse to land in the desired lead. However, some hunters have difficulty doing lead changes on the ground and so must do them in the air. To do a change in the air, look where you want to go, use your opening rein in the new direction, shift your weight slightly in the new direction, and place your outside calf against the horse's side. If you want to land on the left lead, for example, look left, use a left opening rein in midair, and squeeze with your right leg.

You can introduce this concept in your flatwork sessions. Place a pole on the ground and canter in a twenty-meter circle on the right lead. As you approach the ground pole, look left. Use a left opening rein as your horse takes the final canter stride at the base of the pole. The timing of your aids is crucial. At the moment of suspension, when she's actually over the pole, squeeze hard with your right leg as if you're asking for the left lead during a canter depart on the flat. Practice in both directions so your hunter becomes ambidextrous, but don't force the issue and sacrifice the horse's jumping technique.

Here a rider looks right and uses an opening right rein to ask for the lead change as her horse canters over a ground pole.

Putting Your Horse on the Bit

A horse on the bit is a beautiful sight. With his arched neck and upright figure, he looks like a steed straight off an antique carousel. But this figure is much more than a pretty face. When a horse is properly on the bit, he becomes functional to himself and his rider. As he stretches into the bit, his topline muscles come into play; his back lifts, which creates a comfortable seat for his rider and a strong shock-absorbing cushion for his own spine and joints. Being on the bit also gives horse and rider that connection we've all heard so much about. The arched topline connects the haunches to the front end so that the animal moves in one fluid motion, and his rider is able to influence his body more easily and with softer aids.

On the Bit

Riding a horse on the bit feels like riding with super shock absorbers, a potent accelerator, and power brakes and steering. Riding a horse above, behind, or against the bit feels quite the opposite. His hollow back gives a jostling ride, and because his upside-down figure lacks that all-important connection, you won't have any influence over his haunches, and you'll have to resort to using strong aids to slow down, stop, or even accelerate.

Unfortunately, the term *on the bit* has led to confusion and incorrect riding and training. As mentioned above, being on the bit involves not just the horse's head but also his body and even his mind. Uneducated riders, desperate to create that pretty picture, often resort to heavy or seesawing hands, gadgets, or harsh bits. Forcing a horse on the bit is much like forcing a ballerina onto her toes. It may work for a little while, but once the force is taken away, the dancer will be right back to square one. There are no quick fixes when teaching a horse to come on the bit. It takes technique that builds submission, suppleness, and muscles over time.

You can tell if a horse is correctly on the bit by watching from the saddle and on the ground. From the saddle, you should be able to see that the poll is at the highest point of the neck. Because those topline muscles will be working, the crest of your horse's neck should look like a dolphin's back jumping out of the water. You should see that fat, wide shape starting from the pommel of your saddle and ending at the base of the ears. Because your horse is actively holding the bit in his mouth (versus having the bit passively resting inside his mouth), your reins will be stretched evenly.

This horse demonstrates the way the neck arches and the topline is lifted as the horse stretches into the bit.

This lower-level dressage horse shows a beginning stretch into contact, indicating that he is on the bit, though not with the advanced outline expected of a higher level horse.

If you're watching from the ground, you'll be able to see the neck muscles bulge along the top while the bottom muscles hang slack. The crest will look like one long smooth muscle. The horse's neck shouldn't start at the chest and swan upward, like the neck of a teapot. It should come straight out of the withers and arch toward the poll. The poll should be the highest point, with the head just in front of an imaginary vertical line. The horse's figure should be arch shaped rather than L shaped. The haunches should swing freely while taking an easy stride forward.

Just because your horse isn't arched in the neck doesn't exactly mean he's incorrect. There are various degrees of on the bit, and which one your horse is able to carry off depends on his degree of flexibility, training, conformation, and ability. Accepting the bit means that a horse happily stretches into the rider's hand, which is often the case with green, or lower-level, dressage horses, hunters, and jumpers. This beginning stretch will still lift the topline, but the body won't arch as much as the body of an upper-level dressage horse. That more pronounced arch means that the horse has learned to take a bigger step under with his haunches and as a result, his figure is more upright and compact.

Although it's true that some horses are born looking as if they're on the bit, these "uphill" equines haven't cornered the market. All horses can achieve some degree of roundness with training and time. In fact, in the time of the fourth-century B.C. Greek general Xenophon (who wrote the first book on dressage), horses were peasant stock and often built for sturdiness rather than athletic ability.

How to Put a Horse on the Bit

If you think of putting a horse on the bit as the icing on the cake, you can't go far wrong. First, you need to bake that cake, and in this case, the cake is you and your horse's basics. You must have a well-balanced position with independent hands (meaning you don't need them for balance!) and a correct leg position. Your horse must be able to fulfill certain requirements in the training pyramid (see The Training Pyramid, or Scale in chapter 3): rhythm, looseness, and contact.

Here are the steps for putting your horse on the bit:

- Make sure that your horse's neck is straight.
- While in steady contact with both reins, close your lower legs, and ask your horse to take a small step forward.
- You will feel the horse push into the bit. Don't stretch your hands forward to stop the pressure. Instead, keep the same rein length, and softly close your hands.
- Your horse will react either by softening his mouth and stretching to your hand (good) or by pulling or raising his head (not good). If he's softened to your hand, immediately give, which in this case means go back to your original contact.
- If your horse has pulled or raised his head, repeat the question until he softens. This may take a little time if your horse is used to a different way. Be patient.

A hunter/jumper stretches into the bit.

- Now try at the trot (both rising and sitting) and canter. You'll find it's not as easy. If either of you gets confused, come back to a walk and reestablish.

Keep in mind that what you are trying to achieve is a contact. You want your horse to step into the bit and hold it. This contact will feel alive and somewhat spongy. Your responsibility is to hold with sensitivity and a soft feel. Don't pull back, and don't slacken the reins completely. As your horse progresses in his training and as his haunches develop, he'll start taking bigger steps with his hind legs and become more arched in his body.

A rider tests whether her horse is on the bit by giving her reins forward. The horse should stretch into the new contact.

Test: Is Your Horse on the Bit?

There is a tried-and-true method to test whether your horse is on the bit correctly. So trusted is this method that it is included in the dressage tests and is awarded double points. In training, it's called the forward, downward stretch. At the walk or trot, give your arms slowly forward, playing out the reins as much as your horse will take. If he doesn't stretch or if he yanks the reins out of your hands, he has not been on the bit. If he starts to stretch a little, you're on the right track. If he follows your stretch completely, moving toward the ground while keeping his topline arched, you're right on the money. During this stretch, your horse's back should feel very swingy and elastic. He should feel better than he did when you began your ride. Also, since forward, downward is a comfortable stretch for a horse, you'll hear him snort and blow and take deep sighs.

Here a dressage rider proves her horse is nicely on the bit by releasing the reins while riding a circle at the trot.

Troubleshooting

A horse may fail to come on the bit for many, various reasons. As mentioned earlier, a horse must fill several requirements before he's physically able to come on the bit. And a rider has to have sound basics as well. But if you've got a horse that is determined to have his own way, there are other things to try.

Horses that pull or come above the bit do so to push their haunches out behind them. You can ask your horse to bow his neck for you, but if the connection from the haunches isn't there, you'll be wasting your time. Because it's very difficult to keep your seat if a horse is pulling, the best place to retrain your horse is on the lunge. Make sure to adjust the side reins so that your horse can put his nose slightly in front of the vertical. Spend most of your time working at the trot and canter, as this is where you'll find the most resistance.

When a horse is above the bit, as here, the topline is no longer arched, and the bottom neck muscle is apparent.

As your horse tries to pull or come above the bit, encourage him to take a longer step forward by swinging the lunge whip at his haunches. He'll soon discover that it's no use pulling; he's only pulling against himself. And if he's coming above the bit, the side reins will catch him every time.

This horse's overbent neck (note that the poll is not the highest point) indicates that he is behind the bit.

In addition to pulling or coming above the bit, another common evasion is coming behind the bit. Horses prone to coming behind the bit are often built with very good conformation or a slighter throat-latch than the average horse, which makes it easier to roll the head down. Unfortunately, it's hard to tell the horse is behind the bit because the contact feels so light. Your first tip-off will be a constant need to reel in the reins. There's also a visual clue. Your horse's poll will not be the highest point. Instead, his neck will have a shrimplike curl to it, with the highest point being the third vertebrae. And as with a horse that pulls, this resistance isn't just in the neck. A horse behind the bit will stop stepping through with his haunches. He'll often have a look or feel as though he is moving or hovering in place.

You can correct this bad habit by driving your horse forward with your legs, at the same time tapping one rein in an upward forward motion to encourage him to push his nose out. You can also put your horse on the lunge with side reins and push him on with your lunge whip when he tries to "suck back."

A rider works her horse on a lunge line and side reins to improve the contact with the bit.

If you have a horse that has been badly trained and has learned to pull against you, you may have to put some might on your side. The controversy over gadgets and their place in the horse world continues to rage. Purists say their only place is in the trash can, others say they can help in certain circumstances, and some won't leave home without them. The consensus is that if you have to reach for a gadget, you've got a problem. It's better to go back in your training and review basics first. However, if you're unsure, always use a training aid temporarily and under the supervision of a knowledgeable person. Gadgets in the wrong hands can create more problems than they solve.

Once your horse understands how to come on the bit, you'll feel as though you've been given a new improved version. He'll feel supercharged and extracomfortable.

Riding Figures

Correctly ridden figures are the hallmarks of good riding. Dressage tests consist of one figure after the next, such as a turn across the diagonal followed by a ten-meter circle. And courses are really no more than school figure patterns with jumps. Figures not only test your skills as a rider—understanding geometry, timing and correct use of the aids, and keeping your horse under control as you turn—but also test your horse's basic training. Think about it: if you can't get your horse to go from point A to point B in some sort of organized fashion, you're missing vital rudiments. Properly ridden, figures also diagnose problems in your horse's training. Let's say you can't get your horse to make a change of rein out of a circle. The problem could be balance or bend or even submission. Figures give you somewhere to start to evaluate your training. One of the best side effects of school figures is greater flexibility because figures require a horse to use her body properly. But to benefit from figures, you first have to ride them correctly. Let's review the aids.

The Mechanics of Turning

Your horse is built long and narrow, just like a bicycle. We all know that it takes very little effort to turn a bike or push it off balance. You don't turn a bike by wrenching on the handlebars; wherever you look, along with a gentle touch on the handlebars, is where you'll go. This happens because when you turn your head and the direction of your eyes, your weight follows. That shift in equilibrium affects the bike's direction. This same shift influences your horse because she feels most balanced with her

This balanced dressage rider demonstrates the correct use of aids as she and her horse turn.

long and narrow body centered beneath her cargo. And if a horse can feel the tiniest fly land on her coat, she'll certainly feel your stability change.

The horse's narrow build also means that she has to use her neck as a balancing pole. If you interfere with that balancing pole, say, by pulling the horse's neck in the direction of your turn, you'll actually force her to balance in other ways, such as leaning on one shoulder or falling in or out. If you've ever ridden a young horse, you've probably noticed that she feels very "wiggly" and looks unsettled in her outline. That's because she's using her neck, along with leaning on her shoulders, to help figure out how to balance the weight of the rider. To train that young horse, you help her learn to balance by keeping her neck straight and pushing her forward while using a leading rein to turn. If you grab the inside rein to turn that young horse, you'll find that you've made the problem worse and that you're suddenly riding an overbent horse going in the wrong direction.

Here a rider demonstrates how pulling her horse's head causes the horse to lean on a shoulder for balance.

So it's your responsibility to keep the horse's balance in mind through the turn. Forget about turning her head—her legs, not her nose, are on the ground, and the legs are what you've got to turn while keeping her balancing pole (her neck) straight.

Dance partners have to follow each other; otherwise, they look as though they are each doing their own thing. The same cooperation is required of you and your horse if you want to achieve that flowing communication and partnership. Here's the rule: your shoulders must parallel your horse's shoulders, and your hips must parallel your horse's hips. This means inside shoulder back, outside shoulder forward, outside hip back (which also causes the outside leg to move behind the girth and helps keep the haunches from swinging out), and inside hip forward (which also causes your inside leg to come a bit forward, which helps with inside leg to outside rein). This is a nice concept on paper, but putting it in practice is another matter. Instead, think of pointing your inside hip and the buttons on your shirt in the direction you want to go. You'll end up with the required parallels.

Here are the steps to turning your horse properly:

- Look up and find your target out of the corner of your eye (don't turn your head or shoulders until you are ready to turn).
- Alert your horse to the turn by flexing her head in the new direction with gentle squeezes on the inside rein. Half halt the outside rein so she understands that the turn isn't happening yet.
- A few steps before the turn (the number of steps will be determined by how large or small or nimble your horse is), begin to bring your outside leg back and your inside leg forward (think of pointing the inside hip).
- A step or two before the mark, turn your head and shoulders (think buttons turning), apply your inside leg to outside rein aid, and turn. Because turns bleed off energy, you may also want to add your driving aid to encourage your horse to push through with forward motion.

- Finish the turn by equaling the pressure in both reins, straightening the horse's head, sitting forward, and bringing both legs back to the girth.

Diagonal Aids

The incorrect or lack of use of the diagonal aids, often called riding with your inside leg to outside hand aid, is a common issue for many riders. This aid is extremely important when riding figures, for many reasons. The aid helps balance or rebalance a horse and is used while bending and while straightening. It's also examined in some of the dressage tests, when the rider is asked to give the inside rein on the circle. The judge wants to see that the horse can maintain her balance on the figure without her rider holding her there with the inside rein;

This rider keeps her horse balanced with the proper use of the inside leg to outside rein aid.

she remains bent because of the rider's correct use of the inside leg to the outside rein aid.

It doesn't really matter which comes first, the leg aid or the rein aid, but suffice it to say that one always immediately follows the other: a light squeeze of the inside leg and then a slight squeeze on the outside rein (or vice versa). The aid lasts momentarily (long enough to say *elephant*) and is repeated if needed. Riders go wrong when they forget to use one or the other. If you use only your leg, the horse will think you want her to go forward and will respond with speed; if you use only your rein, your horse will think you want to slow down and will respond in kind. The two work together to use the horse's energy, generated by your leg and directed by your hand, to balance the horse. In simpler terms, the outside rein prevents the horse from falling out, and the inside leg prevents her from falling in.

Here is a quick review of the use of diagonal aids:

- inside leg just at the girth
- outside leg just behind the girth
- shoulders turned toward the inside of the figure
- slight flexion (turning the horse's head only; you should just see her eye) with the inside rein and a steady contact on the outside rein.

With smaller figures, increase the turn of your shoulders to the inside. If you have trouble turning your shoulders, look at your horse's inside hip. That's how much you should bring your shoulder back.

Many riders often assume a horse is bent because her neck is bent. Remember that the neck is the horse's balancing pole and for the most part must remain straight through the bend. The horse should bend through her body and not her neck—this is where your diagonal aids come into use. She should flex at the poll only. Watch a horse scratch her barrel, and you'll see that she can easily bend her neck without bending her body.

School Figure Tips

There are many school figures; however, the serpentine, circles, and interlinking circles are the three most commonly chosen. The serpentine is a very valuable pattern. It shows your ability to balance and bend your horse—and your horse's ability to bend and balance—and your readiness to move on to greater skills such as counter canter, flying changes, and lateral work. To ride a serpentine well, all the loops have to be equal and must have an appropriate bend in each direction with no loss of rhythm (correct pattern of footfalls for that gait) or tempo (speed) when changing from one direction to the next. Your horse has to cross the centerline parallel to the short side and perpendicular to the centerline. The whole pattern must appear to flow.

The standard three-loop serpentine consists of three linked twenty-meter circles. Know where each twenty-meter circle starts and ends, and you can visualize how the serpentine falls. Begin your serpentine at either A or C. Keep in mind that you will ride into the corner on the approach to the serpentine and after you finish it, but you will arc out on the second and third corners because they will be incorporated in your loops. To change the direction toward the next loop, you must ride across the centerline straight for at least three strides before turning into the new direction, during which time you change the flexion and the bend of your horse. Touch the wall for one stride only (do not ride along the wall) and arc off to finish the loop.

Fifteen-meter circles and ten-meter circles are used to determine many things from both rider and horse. These are used to test balance and responsiveness and to determine if the horse responds to the rider's aids, rather than just ricocheting off the sides of the arena, as can happen in a twenty-meter circle. The circles demand turnability, which means mobility of the forehand. In practice, the smaller circles are useful in evaluating the rider's accuracy and ability to turn the horse properly and not just drag her around by the mouth.

When riding a serpentine, this pair creates the loops while avoiding riding into the corners.

When making turns and circles, it is important to remember that, mechanically if not visually, the horse makes a circle as a polygon. Cultivate the simple turn responses before trying to demonstrate the final version of a smooth circle. Turn sharply enough from the track to start the circle, ride a step or two straight, turn again when you've made a quarter of the circle, go straight for a step or two, turn when you've made half of the circle, and repeat. During this exercise, check for *self-carriage* frequently. Self-carriage means that your horse is not relying on your reins to prop herself up. To test for this, loosen the reins for several strides. Your horse should remain balanced and move at the same tempo.

Practice ten-meter circles by starting with eight-meter circles and leg yielding out (see chapter six) to create the ten-meter circle. This will improve bend, balance, and fluency. It also gives you hedging room at the show in case your horse doesn't turn as well or drifts out. You have two meters to turn as well as you'd like.

The two interlinking half ten-meter circles ridden across the school from E to X and from X to B (that occur in First Level dressage tests) demonstrate the quality of bend and balance on a circle and the change of bend in balance. The most common fault is loss of balance and carriage at the moment of change of direction at X. For the horse to change both bend and direction requires some major changes and retooling of her equilibration system and of the locomotor system. The difficulty for the rider is to change the bend before changing the direction.

Because this movement requires specific preparation and response, there is a lot a rider can do to make it work. On the first circle—let's say going to the left from E—well before reaching the centerline, the rider should begin to ask for flexion in the throatlatch to the new direction (right), and leg yield to the left. The turn to the right should not be effected until the horse leg yields left with right flexion. In the teaching stage, this should be done in an obvious way. In the performance stage, the horse will have the general idea, and the rider can ask more subtly.

A horse and rider are showing a good bend in the first circle of the interlocking half ten-meter circles pattern.

The horse is balanced as the circle continues, and the rider looks forward to the next circle.

All flatwork sessions should finish off with the twenty-meter stretching circle to check that the horse's balance, contact, and connection during the workout were good and genuine and to stretch and relax the horse's back.

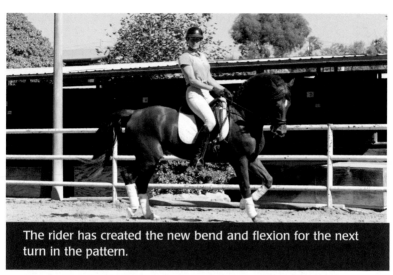

The rider has created the new bend and flexion for the next turn in the pattern.

The good bend and balance continue throughout the second circle.

6

Lateral Work

Many riders, in particular dressage riders, strive to master lateral work. Not only does lateral work make a pretty picture, but correctly done, it also demonstrates that the basic training of the horse has been achieved and that the work is moving in the right direction. But lateral work is more than this. It teaches the rider how to keep the horse straight and how to use the diagonal aids correctly. Lateral work increases the horse's engagement (shoulder-in, haunches-in, and half pass) and loosens the shoulders (shoulder-in and half pass), and leg yielding loosens the horse's back.

Suppling Exercises

Suppling a horse is an important concept at all levels of English riding. For a horse to remain sound throughout his life, he must remain flexible.

Leg Yielding

Leg yielding is one exercise that will help achieve suppleness. In the test, it also shows obedience and correctness of the horse's response to the rider's influences. It is not only an exercise in and of itself but also a tool for circles, corners, and turn-on-the-forehand, and it narrows the horse's base of support for better balance. In the leg yield, the horse moves in a forward, sideways movement, slightly bent away from the direction of travel.

The most common problem in leg yielding is lack of alignment; usually the horse's neck is twisted at the withers. The horse's body

For a correct leg yield, the horse must be bent slightly away from the direction of travel, as shown.

parts—neck and main body—should all be aligned. To avoid alignment problems, wait until you've straightened out of your turn before you begin to leg yield. Then ask your horse for a slight flexion in the opposite direction of travel by squeezing the rein (for instance, the right rein if you're moving toward the left) until you see a little bit of your horse's eye. Use your diagonal aids as you ask for the leg yield, but make sure to half halt adequately on the outside rein (if you're moving in that direction) as you ask for the leg yield; otherwise, your horse will keep moving forward and not sideways. The key here is to displace the horse's energy sideways. Look up, find a spot on the wall to ride to, and think "a step forward, a step sideways" as you ride the leg yield. To the spectator, your horse should appear to be straight and moving sideways energetically, with his legs crossing and uncrossing.

Turn-on-the-Forehand

Although turn-on-the-forehand has no gymnastic value, the turn-on-the-forehand can teach both horse and rider how to use and respond to the very important basics of inside leg to outside rein. It can also help a horse understand how you'd like him to use his haunches. It is useful when you want a horse to move sideways—away from another horse or into a fence you'd like to open while mounted. Your horse should move away from your inside leg aid and into the outside rein, neatly crossing his inside leg over his outside leg, all the while keeping the same tempo as he makes the turn. Even though you'll remain in one spot, your horse should keep his energy up while making the turn. He should step around his front legs, which will continue to stay in motion, stepping a little bit forward while turning about.

This exercise is often mistakenly started from a halt, which causes problems. If you're rooted to the spot, your horse's haunches will stop stepping underneath, and the result will be the circus pony pivot. Therefore, approach it from the walk. Walk down the long

A horse and rider begin a turn-on-the-forehand.

side of your school. Apply a half halt, and slow your horse's walk momentarily. As you feel him shorten his stride, flex his head slightly toward the wall, bending him a little to the outside. Bring your inside leg behind the girth, and apply your outside leg at the girth. Now half halt the inside rein again, then use your outside leg to ask your horse to cross his outside hind leg over to create the turn-on-the-forehand. Each time you apply your outside leg, immediately half halt with your inside rein. (A brief note: This is that all-important basic aid of inside leg to outside rein. We've reversed it here to outside leg to inside rein because we want to use the wall of the school to prevent the horse from barging through your half halt.) When you finish the exercise, move off in the new direction and repeat from the new rein on the other long side.

Two-Track Movements

Two-track movements are so called because they require the horse's body to travel on two different paths. The shoulder-in asks the horse to bend toward one side yet continue moving in another. The haunches-in and out (travers and renvers), half pass, and turn-on-the-haunches ask the horse to move in the direction of his bend. The aids are all the same for this second group of movements; only the intensity of the aid varies.

The Shoulder-Fore and the Shoulder-In

The shoulder-in is one of the most challenging of the lateral movements. It is the first time the horse is asked to bring his hips closer together, flex his hocks, and swing his shoulders to one side. In dressage, it is the preparation for all other lateral exercises. It is beneficial in other disciplines because it teaches a horse straightness, which helps create balance, and it supples his body, which makes carrying a rider easier.

Shoulder-fore is the precursor to the shoulder-in. Shoulder-fore has a lesser degree of angle and bend. The aids are the same but are used with less intensity. It's best to teach the horse this movement first; once the horse understands how to flex his hocks, the angle can be increased. When you teach a horse shoulder-in, he often doesn't understand and will give a steep angle, similar to a leg yield. It's easy for him to swing his shoulders but harder for him to carry his weight in his hocks. So angle isn't better when approaching a shoulder-in.

For both the shoulder-in and shoulder-fore, your inside leg should be at the girth to maintain lateral bend. Your outside leg is behind the girth to stop the haunches from falling out. Flex your horse to the inside, and make your outside rein more solid to support the bend and help your horse stay on the track. Sit slightly to the inside with more weight on the inside seat bone; you achieve angle in this movement by turning your upper body. Your horse will learn this means to bring his forehand in. Increase the turning of your body,

A horse and rider school the shoulder-in.

and the horse will increase the angle to create the shoulder-in. Most people can't feel the shoulder-fore, so it is helpful to ask someone on the ground to point out how far you are leaving the track.

Use your corner to establish a bend before you begin. Then send your horse down the long side in a shoulder-in or a shoulder-fore. You can also ride a small circle to establish the bend, then ride the movement out of it. Try the smaller angle for a few strides, bring your horse back to the track, brighten the gait, and increase the angle to shoulder-in. Finish the movement by straightening the shoulders with your outside rein, pushing your inside leg against the horse's side, turning your body forward, and riding straight ahead.

Haunches-In

Haunches-in (also called travers) is the most advanced way to teach your horse inside bend. For a correct haunches-in, your horse must move with his front legs and shoulders on the track and his haunches off the track (haunches-out, also called renvers, requires a horse to move with his shoulders off the track and his haunches on the track). Sit facing straight ahead with your shoulders aligned with your horse's shoulders. Keep your inside leg at the girth (calf supports the bend and keeps the horse at the track) and your outside leg behind the girth (pressure from your calf asks the haunches to swing in). The outside rein helps keep the horse's neck straight, and the inside rein asks for a slight flexion to the inside. Keep more weight on the inside sitting bone. Your horse's neck and shoulders should be parallel to the long side, and the rest of his body should be bent to the inside.

Horses often lean to the wall, so ask for the haunches-in on the centerline or quarterline instead. If you're getting a lot of neck bend, you're probably using your reins in place of proper leg aids. Check your aids and try again. Remember to keep the neck and shoulders straight. If you have trouble maintaining the bend, start the haunches-in from a circle to create the bend, then ride straight ahead in haunches-in. Return to the circle if you lose your bend.

The Half Pass

The half pass is a collected movement that demonstrates the horse is supple enough to move forward while bent in the direction of travel, with good balance and at the correct tempo. As a horse moves through the levels, the bend becomes steeper, and the movement travels a greater distance. The half pass develops out of the leg yield and the shoulder-in. The aid for the half pass is to begin in shoulder-fore, then half halt the outside rein to bring the horse over in a half pass. You should sit a little bit more toward the bend.

A horse and rider school the half pass with the help of a ground pole.

Riders often get caught up in producing an angle and end up getting the wrong response. Imagine riding haunches-in on the diagonal instead. Line up four poles in a row on the long diagonal from F. Ride a straight line from F to the first pole, then ride a slight angle (from haunches-in) on the first pole, and finally ride an increased angle on the last three poles. Don't just take any old angle. Be aware of what your horse is giving you. To ride the half pass from start to finish, turn down the centerline at A on the left rein. Remain straight until you reach D, where you will ride your shoulder-fore in preparation. Next, pretend the poles are set from D to E, and ride haunches-in along those imaginary poles. Start with a gradual angle, and once you feel the horse is forward and the bend is good, increase the angle. At the end, if your horse starts to weaken, increase the forward and decrease the angle. It's the same philosophy as in the shoulder-in.

The Turn-on-the-Haunches

The turn-on-the-haunches is a gymnastic exercise, meaning it develops the horse's body. The exercise engages the horse's hindquarters by teaching him how to shorten his body and bring the haunches closer to the front end. It's difficult to feel what's going on with the haunches at the walk, and because of the slower pace, horses can be very evasive. Therefore, ask a friend on the ground to watch you until you get the hang of it.

The essence of turn-on-the-haunches is that the horse marches around his inside hind hoof. His inside hind hoof should step in place while the outside hoof and front hooves move around it. The horse's hind hooves should stay in the center of the circle, and his body should move around the periphery. Your horse should move in a pure walk with a good four-beat rhythm and a steady tempo. He should remain balanced and on the bit, looking and bending in the direction of travel. The exercise should begin and end in the same spot.

This is the first step in a turn-on-the-haunches: the rider asks for a slight half pass.

Step 2 in the turn-on-the-haunches: the rider uses her outside rein and leg to prepare the horse to turn his forehand around the haunches.

The horse begins to turn his forehand while his outside hind leg steps around the inside hind leg. The inside foreleg should march in place.

Walk down the centerline, and ride a leg yield to the right for a few strides. When you feel your horse step into and fill the outside rein, change your mind and ride in the other direction (leg yield toward the bend). This will give you a baby half pass. If all is well and he's moving nicely forward and sideways, half halt your outside rein, and apply your outside leg. Sit to the inside, and follow the horse's body around with your body as he turns. Each time you make another step in the turn, apply another driving aid with your inside leg, another half halt, and another turning aid with your outside aids: drive, half halt, turn, drive, half halt, turn. Keep in mind that most of the control of the turn is done with your outside rein and leg. You'll guard his outside hindquarters with your outside aids to keep him from falling out of the turn. Your inside leg will keep the bend and tell him to keep those haunches moving while the inside rein maintains the flexion. Don't ask for too much at once. Make a quarter turn, move forward for a bit, and then repeat the exercise.

Cavalletti
and Ground Poles

Problems encountered during jumping or dressage can be overcome by using cavalletti and ground poles. For dressage horses, cavalletti and ground poles are great for improving the walk, the trot, and the balance; they benefit the action of a horse's motion and increase suspension. Hunters and jumpers also learn balance, but more important, cavalletti and ground poles teach the horse how to jump without stressing joints. For all horses, cavalletti and ground poles are beneficial for overall rideability, control, and fitness. This type of work teaches the jumper rider to learn the all-important distance from jump to jump and teaches the dressage rider balance and feel.

Cavalletti, Italian for "little jump," was invented in the early 1800s by Italian cavalry officer Captain Federico Caprilli, also the founder of the forward seat and the theory of training by natural methods. Caprilli used horizontal poles on low stands to improve horses' balance as they rode over the poles at different gaits. Cavalletti work soon became a familiar concept in all Italian cavalry schools. Today, cavalletti is a respected and valuable exercise throughout the world in all disciplines.

Cavalletti is a variation on a theme of simple horizontal rails. The rails are arranged in series, resting on plastic or wooden end blocks or permanently fixed to an X that can be turned to various heights. Consider your height settings carefully. The closer together

A hunter/jumper pair confidently trots over cavalletti.

cavalletti are, the lower they should be, although the top height of the X-style cavalletti is fine for canter. Ground poles simply rest on the ground and are a substitute for cavalletti. Since they aren't fixed, they can be easily kicked or stepped on, so use heavy poles that can't be dislodged easily. Cavalletti and ground poles should be 2 feet, 8 inches to 3 feet for the walk, 3 to 4½ feet apart for trot work, and 9 to 12 feet apart for canter work. (All stride lengths depend upon the horse's stride and the exercise.)

Cavalletti and ground poles can be ridden at all three gaits. It's easier to stay in balance by riding over the objects in the rising trot. If a rider isn't very secure in the saddle, jumping position is another option. Jumping position also gets the rider's weight off the horse's back, which is a good choice if a horse is green and uncertain about her footing over cavalletti. Aim to ride across the center of the poles and look straight ahead.

The horse should be able to cross the obstacles on the lunge before he carries a rider over them. Outfit your horse with brushing

A horse is wearing side reins to help her learn to move through the unfamiliar cavelletti without hollowing her back and inverting her neck.

boots and bell boots for protection, and attach side reins. Many horses new to cavalletti will move through in a hollow posture; the side reins, properly fitted so that the horse's nose is slightly in front of the vertical, will keep the horse stretching into the bit contact.

Many horses worry about something new, so introduce the exercise by leading the horse over a pole on the ground, then add two more poles on a little curve, set at a trot stride. If all is well, begin to lunge the horse through this grid at the walk (without side reins so you won't restrict the horse's head and neck) and then at the trot (with side reins attached). Three poles are better than two because horses are more inclined to jump over two poles rather than trot through them. As your horse gets used to the exercise, add more poles; a total of five to seven will challenge your horse sufficiently.

Exercises for Hunters and Jumpers

Trotting over rails teaches the horse how to raise her shoulders and keep her head and neck in a steady position prior to jumping. They also keep the horse balanced and attentive, and they give the rider a focal point. Set up this exercise by using the X-style cavalletti turned to the lowest position, using poles on the ground, or using poles set in holders. Use three to six poles set about four feet apart (again, depending on the stride of the horse). Ride through in a steady trot, aiming for the center of the poles. To add to this exercise, include a small jump eight feet away, which is one trotting stride, as you will be jumping out of the trot and not the canter.

Canter cavalletti prompts the horse to use her back muscles and encourages her to relax, slow down, and listen to her rider. As she canters over the X-style cavalletti (which can be elevated to the top height), she pushes into the bit contact and stretches her neck. You can increase the difficulty by pairing two cavalletti to make an oxer. Place another pair about eighteen feet away. Canter over the first oxer, trot in the middle, and canter over the second oxer.

A small jump has been added to the end of the row of ground poles, one trotting stride from the last pole.

Developing an eye for jumping stride is a skill that can be learned over canter cavalletti. Set two cavalletti at one stride followed by a third set at double (for example, if you choose to set your canter cavalletti at twelve feet apart, the double distance will be twenty-four feet). The horse will canter over the first two obstacles in her stride, then take one full stride before cantering over the third. You can then triple the distance to the third pole for a two stride, and quadruple it for a three stride. You'll soon gain the sense of how many strides are required in a certain distance; all you need to do is keep a steady rhythm and let the horse carry you through the pattern. To learn to lengthen and shorten a horse's stride within a combination, which is often required in show jumping, add more cavalletti at odd distances, such as a forward two stride of thirty-eight feet, rather than the steady thirty-six feet for a two stride; or decrease the distance to thirty-four feet for a shortened two stride.

A dressage rider schools her horse at the canter between the cavalletti to work on transitions and create forward energy.

Exercises for the Dressage Horse

A good exercise to help get the horse more forward and rhythmic in the trot and to improve suppleness and obedience is to ride a figure eight of 2 twenty-meter circles. Place four ground poles or X-style cavalletti on the first circle in a curved row, about 4½ feet apart. Trot through the poles on one rein, complete the circle, then change rein and ride the second twenty-meter circle to create the figure eight. You can increase the difficulty by picking up a canter as you enter the second circle and then coming back to the trot just before you ride through.

To create a more forward horse, place five to seven cavalletti or ground poles in a series about 4½ to 5 feet apart. Trot over the poles, and pick up a canter immediately after exiting. This exercise also teaches the rider how to prepare transitions and keep the horse on the aids.

To teach a horse to lengthen stride, place five cavalletti or ground poles 5½ feet apart. Trot through and encourage your horse to take a bigger stride by driving more with your leg. After exiting the grid, make a ten-meter circle in collected sitting trot. Enlarge the circle to twenty meters, then lengthen stride through the grid again.

Canter cavalletti for dressage horses has little benefit because the desired canter in dressage is a canter that moves in an uphill manner. Canter cavalletti often encourages the horse to lengthen and drop her forehand instead of raise it.

Gridwork

Gridwork, also called gymnastic jumping, is a highly useful way of improving your horse's technique and developing his strength. It consists of grids made up of a number of obstacles set in a line to form an alley or a grouping of fences. The grid teaches the horse to think for himself, to jump quietly, and to manage his balance and stride. Gridwork also prevents the horse from grabbing control and rushing the fences. The horse can also learn to hold his line as he jumps. For instance, if he is drifting to the left or right, rather than correct him with your hand, you can cross the poles to encourage him to aim for the middle or set them on the ground before, between, or after the fence. Or you can set them on top of the poles to form a miniature chute. Gridwork also gives the rider the opportunity to concentrate on her own position and technique.

There are many ways to design a grid: you can introduce bounces, teach a horse how to shorten and lengthen his stride, and teach fundamentals of jumping combinations. The height of the fences is not important; the idea is to educate, not to see how big a horse can jump. Therefore, set your fences anywhere from two feet to three feet, three inches.

Always ride the turn to the grid properly to achieve the straightest approach possible. Keep that straightness over the fences and after you land. Many riders make the mistake of allowing the horse to land and then canter off sloppily. When you land, continue in a straight line for a few strides, and then make your turn or transition. Keep your position balanced and quiet throughout, and never interfere with your horse's jump. Instead, try to let the grid do the job for you.

When doing grid exercises, build each grid gradually, starting with one or two elements. You can assemble the entire grid in advance; place the poles and jump cups on the ground on the outside of the fence. Gridwork is also very strenuous, so adjust your time to your horse's fitness level. Often, five or six passes are enough.

The No-Surprises Grid

This exercise is called the no-surprises grid because it puts the horse and rider in the right place for each jump. It is perfect for building confidence. Set up three to five trot ground poles, followed by a jump set one trot stride, about eight to nine feet away. Place two bounces about ten feet away from each other. Set up another fence on a one stride and the final fence on a two stride. Equip all jumps

Here is an example of a no-surprises grid with crossed poles.

A horse and rider approach an angled vertical after jumping an oxer in the no-surprises grid.

with crossed poles at the beginning so that the horse will have to aim for the middle of each fence. As the exercise progresses and your horse and you become more confident, you can change the last fence to an oxer, which will give the horse height and width to bascule over. You can also change the second to last fence into a vertical to make it more challenging.

To work on leads and lead changes, you can add to the no-surprises grid by using two verticals, angled to the right and left of the grid, three or five strides away from the oxer—the pattern will resemble a martini glass. If your horse lands on the left lead, you go over the left vertical; if he lands on the right lead, you go over the right. This teaches the rider to identify which lead the horse has landed on. To advance the exercise, you can change leads in the air and pop over whichever vertical you choose.

Incorporating Placing Poles and Cavalletti

Poles on the ground help improve technique. Inexperienced horses, which lack strength, have a tendency to get lazy after the first two fences, and you may find they flatten over the third. You can put placing poles down in the middle of each fence so that the horse will have to stretch himself as he jumps. If your horse is the type that acts up as he lands, put a pole nine feet away from the last fence to make him pay attention. If he drifts, set up two guide poles on top of the rails of the fence (to create a type of chute) so that the horse's only choice is to jump in the middle. Placing poles, positioned just slightly out from the bottom of the fence, help a horse that tends to get too close. When such a horse sees the pole, he backs off and takes off in the appropriate place. Poles set alongside the grid, in between the jumps, discourage runouts. You can even shorten the distance between the poles to make a chute on the ground.

Here, the placing poles in front of the fences help teach the horse when to jump.

If your horse rushes his fences, you can place a line of cavalletti in a curve in front of a grid of jumps. This will make him pay attention to where he puts his feet and concentrate on his rider.

In and Outs

In and outs (or bounces) improve the action of the horse's back, develop strength, and teach the horse to slow down, sit back on his haunches, lift his front end, and tuck his front legs. Bounce gridwork is very strenuous, so hold your passes to a minimum. Set a placing pole nine feet in front of a grid of no more than five bounces set at ten-foot intervals—start with two bounces. Sit still and let the jump come to you. If your horse handles the bounces well, add another. Try to keep a steady speed into the grid. If you canter too fast into the exercise, you may drop a rail. What has happened is that your horse has tried to shorten himself to get his legs out of the way, which will cause him to come down early and pull rails.

Cross-Country Jumping

Most riders take up eventing because of the cross-country phase. The thrill of speed and the excitement of tackling different fences and obstacles, along with that ever-lurking element of danger, is what draws many people to the sport. But it's a mistake to think that riding cross-country is a free-for-all, a mad dash to gallop over fences in the proper time allowed. Cross-country riding is all about skill, endurance, strength, and nerves of steel.

Cross-Country Basics

In a good cross-country ride, both horse and rider share the same goal—to jump the fence successfully—but each has her own part to play. The rider must have a good position and balance in the saddle, the right mental reactions, and the right attitude. The horse must be forward thinking and maintain her own balance. It's the horse's job to jump the fence, not the rider's. The horse must always maintain that forward enthusiasm and her own balance without always relying on the rider. The horse must learn to stay on line and not to drift.

You must have the best possible control of the horse and be in the most secure position so that when something goes wrong, you will be able to react quickly and remain safe. For cross-country, sit a fraction behind the point of balance, with the center of gravity above the stirrup, which is shortened and placed slightly more forward than usual.

A cross-country rider maintains a good balance and position at the gallop.

This places you in a "safety first" position. The stability of your leg is also very important. Your weight should press down into the stirrup; never cling with the knee, which will cause your heel to swing back. The length of stirrup means you can be clear of the saddle, which will help your horse gallop more freely. Yet when approaching and jumping the fence, your seat should be as close to the saddle as possible.

The seat and lower leg position is constant, but your upper-body position will change for each type of cross-country jump. It can fluctuate between being very forward over a steeplechase fence to leaning back extremely when you jump into water with a drop on the landing side.

This is a good position for cross-country: the rider's seat is close to the saddle, and her hands are in contact but are still allowing the horse freedom to jump.

Your hand should maintain a contact with the horse's mouth, but that contact is often a challenge. Focus on keeping the connection between your hand and the horse's mouth, but without interfering with the jump.

You also have to keep the horse on line and approach the fence in a good rhythm so that the length of the horse's stride remains the same, whatever you have set for that fence, and at the relevant speed for that fence. It may be on a short stride for something like a rail, ditch, rail combination (also called the coffin), or it may be on a longer stride for a steeplechase fence (see chapter 3, Riding Within the Gaits). Whatever rhythm you set, try to maintain it as evenly as possible.

Cross-Country Fences

Few riders are lucky enough to have cross-country fences at home, but any rider can simulate fences. If you have a small arena or you lack cross-country jumps, you can still set up a course worthy of schooling. For small arenas, create jumps that can be ridden in several ways. These jumps will also help improve your turning and jumping at angles. For cross-country fences, you can use several of the show jumping fences, such as the water tray and the corner, and modify them to resemble cross-country courses. Coffins can be duplicated by schooling over oxers. If you have a nice stretch of field at your disposal, you can also set up permanent fences, such as a grid with a small ditch, some bounces, and a brush jump in the distance. These can be simple post-and-rail constructions.

You can use your water pan to duplicate a Trakhener fence or a ditch. You can also place the water pan on its own or in the middle of a combination. This will get you and your horse used to jumping objects without wings.

How much cross-country schooling a horse needs depends on the horse. Some horses will jump into space if pointed that way, and others are more cautious. But with good training, a horse will offer what you want as opposed to your having to hold the whole thing together.

Corners

The golden rule of jumping corners is to bisect the angle of the jump and meet that line straight without turning to jump it at the last second. The horse must maintain the line instead of taking the easy option, which is to duck out to the side, particularly if you are jumping at the extreme end of the fence. Set up a small vertical fence, and begin to jump it from different angles rather than straight on. This will teach your horse to hold her line and not run out. She must be very balanced to jump an angle, lifting both knees equally. Once your horse is very comfortable with this, add another set of standards to create the angle. Place one of the standards in front of another, almost as though you were making an oxer. Do the same on

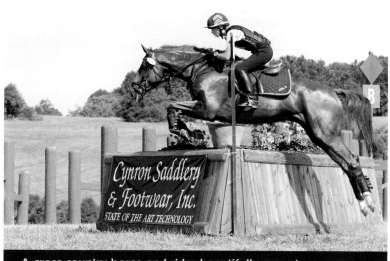

A cross-country horse and rider beautifully execute a corner jump.

the other set, but increase the width a bit. Adding poles will create a corner. Increase the angle and height as your horse gains confidence.

If you are having problems with run-outs, say, at a right-hand corner, come to it at the left lead canter; if your horse wants to run out, she will have to change leads as well.

Ditches

Sometimes the rider is more worried about the ditch than the horse is. This is a psychological obstacle because a horse's stride when she's galloping is at least fifteen feet long: you'll never find a ditch that wide. So you should say to yourself, "If a horse's stride is that long, and a ditch is only that wide, why am I worried?" If your horse is confident about jumping holes in the ground, then don't be worried about the width of the fence.

To jump a ditch, up the tempo, increase the length of stride, and keep coming to it. Don't look for a stride; let the horse judge when to take off. And don't look down into the ditch. As you approach, let the reins slip a little bit longer. Sit more upright in your position, and as you ride to the fence, ride your horse into the contact a little bit. Don't give her a loose rein and allow her to drop her neck and look down into the ditch. On the other hand, don't ride with the reins short and her neck short. If the horse's neck is short, she might feel she can't stretch her neck as she jumps, and so refuse. This advice applies to the open ditch (the ditch in front of a fence) as well as to a ditch without a fence.

The important thing to remember when jumping the rail, ditch, rail combination (coffin) is the spread you come into in the first element. Cut your speed enough to then be riding forward to the rails—there is no point in slowing down further because when the horse suddenly sees the ditch, there is a chance she will stop. Speed is not the cure! Keep an upright posture going in and through so that you are always just behind the horse, ready to react if the horse spooks at the ditch or catches a leg.

A rider maintains the upright position necessary for jumping ditches.

Water

Walk through as much water as you can—walk through puddles when it rains, and splash around in streams you encounter on your trail rides. If you have a stream on your property, walk your horse through it every day. It's most important that your horse learn to trust that the water is not deep and that the ground underneath the water is safe; it's not like quicksand. You shouldn't shake a horse's confidence in the ground; don't take her through good ground one day and bad the next.

Walk into the water first; follow a confident horse into the water if necessary to avoid resistance from your horse. And, of course, giving lots of pats and encouragement is a must. When you're confident that the horse will go in and out of water on her own, increase the difficulty by adding a small drop, such as a log or a small fence, that lands into the water.

Don't school jumping out of water and up a step. There are too many things that can go wrong—your horse can miss the step and cut herself, for instance. A step is OK in competition but not in training. A step is less necessary than a drop, in any case, because all horses will jump out of water, but not all will go in.

As the jump or drop into the water gets bigger, you have to allow the horse's neck more freedom, so ride on a longer rein. If necessary, be prepared to slip the reins through your hands over the jump.

Stay back with your upper body as your horse jumps into the water—don't lean forward—so the horse jumps slightly away from you. Stay upright at least through the first stride in the water, then gradually take a more forward position if, for example, there is a long galloping stretch through the water. On the other hand, if it's only one or two strides followed by another jump out of the water, stay in a more upright position all the way through the water.

Falling off is the worst thing that can happen, and the first stride after the landing is where falling usually occurs. Deep water stops the horse's momentum, and very often the horse will stumble in the water. Modern water jumps are not very deep, so the problem is more often associated with the horse's losing her balance as she drops into the water. Either she's come too forward with her neck or the rider has leaned too far forward on the horse's shoulders, causing her to lose her balance when she takes her first stride. This is why your solid cross-country position is so important.

Drops

If you hold on to your horse's head, she will jump through your hand and jump bigger. If you are jumping a drop, loosen the rein a little bit, and keep your hand down and body back to allow the horse the freedom of her head and neck, so she just pops off the drop. Allow your horse to look down and jump down.

As her horse jumps into the water, this rider stays back with her upper body and allows the reins to slip through her hands and lengthen.

Either the rider lost position or the horse lost balance upon landing a water jump, which usually happens after the first stride in the water. Make sure your position is solid over a water jump.

Banks

Jumping up onto a bank is similar to jumping a vertical fence. Approach it on a very active forward-going stride so the horse has the energy to jump onto it. If you're too fast, the trajectory of the jump will flatten, and your horse won't land up; she'll skid across the step, or she won't land high enough. If you come in too slowly, then the horse will lose her impulsion as she jumps up onto the step, and if there is another obstacle after that, she may not have enough power to jump it.

If you are jumping a derby bank, come quite active up onto it. As you are on top of the bank, your body position should come up and back. Let the reins get longer so the horse can jump off the bank using her neck. You want your horse to jump off some banks or drops very slowly—for example, if there is a jump on the landing stride or the ground runs away on the landing side. In these cases, you want the horse to slide off the bank. So lengthen your rein and reduce the speed to the minimum—almost trot off. However, don't hesitate at the top. Successfully jumping banks means getting that balance of speed right. Many of these situations call for good judgment: getting the right balance of speed, control, forward thought, and freedom and guiding the horse without restriction.

This rider encourages the horse to maintain an active stride while jumping onto a bank.

Cross-country fences are often unusual, such as this duck-shaped water jump. Eventers should be able to jump anything!

Cross-country is really a confidence test between horse and rider—have faith in your horse, and the horse will have faith in you. Don't forget that you are a team and that you should try to work together. When you ride cross-country and your horse sees a fence that she has never encountered before, she'll look to you for help. If you are riding confidently, holding the contact and using your leg, you'll tell her all is well. Even though you might be scared inside, ride confidently.

Hunter Courses

Show hunting originated as a leisure activity many generations ago, when people began to stack their field hunters against one another. The show courses simulate the types of jumps a hunter would encounter in the field. Therefore, the requirements of a good field hunter come into play in the show ring: manners are important because if you are foxhunting on an unruly horse, you can ruin the day for the rest of the riders. A horse with a comfortable gait is desired because a rough-gaited horse makes for an unpleasant ride. A horse that jumps safely is required because if you have a horse with a sloppy jumping style, he can hang a leg on the fence and cause his rider to take a tumble out on the hunt field.

Hunter Basics

To demonstrate these skills, hunters must answer the questions the course asks. For example, each change of direction must be conducted through a flying lead change to show that the horse is handy and balanced. The horse must hit the prescribed level of strides between jumps and ride them evenly and smoothly to demonstrate control. He must take the jump out of his stride, without swapping his leads or chipping in a short stride, to show he's a safe jumper with a good style. All in all, the horse must show the judge a round that flows and meets each jump in stride, turning and jumping from a definite tempo and rhythm.

The misconception about riding hunters is that there is really no skill involved on the rider's part. Many people assume the horse they

This pair exhibits the calm, smooth, controlled jump expected of hunters.

are watching is a "packer," meaning he is doing all the work, regardless of the rider's skill. This is far from the truth. Although it's correct to assume that riding hunters is a rather genteel activity, a great deal of skill is required to achieve that calm, smooth picture. The rider must show that she is in control throughout the round. Therefore, you must be able to judge your distance to each jump, aid the horse in keeping a steady rhythm, and know when to stay out of his way and when to help.

The judge wants to see that you have quiet, sensitive hands and that you aren't relying on the bit for control, so you must keep a quiet contact on the bit between the fences. Over the fence, this contact is relinquished in a crest release, which encourages the horse to stretch his neck out and round himself over the fence to demonstrate that your horse is in perfect control. To do a crest release, place your hands halfway up the horse's neck and on the crest. There should be a noticeable slack or loop in the reins. Equitation riders are different, and instead ride with a soft contact and have more of a following hand, with a straight line from the bit to the rider's elbow, which is similar to a jumper or an event rider. This type of release is called an automatic release.

The hunt seat position, or the two-point position, is held both over the fence and on the flat. In the two-point, the hip angle is

An equitation rider demonstrates the proper form for hunt seat: she keeps a two-point position over the jump but uses an automatic release instead of a crest release.

closed, and the seat bones are out of the saddle. The upper body is slightly ahead of the vertical, which allows you to stay close to the center of gravity. This position encourages the horse to stride forward, and if something goes wrong (say a horse has a deep takeoff spot), you will already be forward and so less likely to get left behind. Also, the two-point is a visual indication of a smooth ride. As the horse jumps there will be a slight closing of your hip angle.

Hunter Fences

Hunter fences are not as complicated or as flashy as eventing and show jumping fences are. The two types of jumps found in hunter courses are verticals and oxers. In lower levels, jumps are usually entirely verticals. Oxers are normally first encountered in the two-foot, six-inch division. Combinations in all classes are ordinarily in and outs.

Verticals

The vertical is typically the first jump on the hunter course. In lines to related jumps, the first effort will be a vertical and the second an oxer. So, for instance, you'll jump into a line over the vertical and canter five or six strides and jump out over an oxer. The vertical fence requires a deeper approach; otherwise, the horse will jump it flatly. This is something that riders often forget to address. Because they want their horses to be soft and flowing freely around the course, they become complacent when jumping the so-called easy, nondescript vertical.

To tune a horse to the vertical, place a ground pole about nine to ten feet in front of the jump (to make a type of bounce combination). Approach it in a working canter; ride over the pole and then over the jump. The pole will put the horse into a position where he has to rock back on his hocks, bring his front end under, and jump out over the vertical. This exercise will also help sharpen your approach to verticals.

An Appaloosa and rider jump a simple vertical.

Oxers

One aspect of a good hunter is scope, the natural ability to jump a wide object. Oxers give the judge the perfect opportunity to evaluate this skill. One element seen on every course is the single oxer, set apart and jumped on a long approach. Here the judge is looking for the horse to stay on the same pace and not switch his lead. However, the lengthy approach has its own risks: For the rider, it's easy to obsess about the jump and the perfect takeoff spot. For the horse, it's easy to break the rhythm and waver off the line.

The key to riding oxers is to make sure you don't take off from a long spot. If you leave from six feet in front of a four-foot-wide oxer, you may not make it to the other side. You don't want your horse reaching the zenith of his arc over the middle of the oxer, with

Oxers such as this one test a horse and rider's ability to jump a wide distance.

This horse is taking off from a good spot—neither long nor deep—which is especially important when jumping oxers.

the dangerous potential of pulling the back rail or having your horse struggle and scramble in an effort to make it across. If, on the other hand, you find you are too deep to the oxer, soften your reins and add leg for more energy. Bottom line: stay out of the horse's way, maintain a rhythm, and don't overthink the takeoff.

Keeping the Flow

Horses should never be quick off the ground when jumping hunter fences. This expression describes a horse that comes to the jump steadily and then, at the moment of takeoff, surges forward and snaps off the ground to get over the jump. The danger here is not only a break in the flow of the ride but also that the horse will have stopped thinking about his technique and will hang his legs and pull rails. Horses that jump like this aren't "patting" the ground on the approach. When a horse pats the ground, he takes the time to come back on his hocks, pick up the front end, and jump. A rider who doesn't trust her horse can create this problem of failing to pat. Because she lacks confidence or is unsure when the horse will leave the ground, she adds leg at the base of the jump. This is one of the big mistakes that can ruin a horse's jumping style or technique. The imperative in hunters is not to just get over the fence but to get over with style. A good hunter rider will wait and add the leg when it's needed. If the horse is flowing and on a nice length of stride, just be quiet and stay still.

Riding the Course

In simplest terms, a hunter course is a series of lines and turns with jumps in the way. It's a flatwork exercise with obstacles. People often forget to pay attention to the flatwork and the basic dressage that is

A pair jumps a combination in a hunter course.

necessary to ride a hunter course well. The problem with focusing on the jumps alone is that you will fail to ride a straight line after an obstacle. You should also consider riding into your corners, with proper bend and on the correct lead. If not, you will ruin your approach to the next jump. When studying the course, take into account where your lead changes will occur. Horses tend to be left- or right-handed, so some will choose which lead they like to land on. If your horse prefers to land on the left, think about jumping out of the line, continuing on, taking your lead change, and making the turn. A smoothly flowing, visually appealing, enjoyable round should be your goal.

Show Jumping Courses

Show jumping has many unique aspects that draw riders of every level and age throughout the world. Many people like the challenge of jumping against the clock, and a rider has to prove himself at every competition: the adage "one day you're tops, and the next you're down" holds very true in this particular English discipline. Even top riders can find themselves winning with one horse and falling off with another in the same class. The sport is also accessible to all levels. Although Grand Prix jumping is what introduces most spectators to the sport, fences start at two feet at the lowest levels.

Show Jumping Basics

Jumpers are often lumped with hunters, but show jumping has more in common with eventing. You don't have to have perfect equitation to compete in show jumping; you need only jump the fence cleanly. That may appear simple, but the truth is that a lot of finesse is required in show jumping. At the lower levels, many riders choose to gallop around the course in carefree abandon. He who runs the fastest can win, but as the fences get higher and higher, the whole formula changes. The level of difficulty rises sharply. You must demonstrate control and ability; otherwise, you will knock down rails or have problems balancing your horse to the next fence.

A horse and rider clear an oxer in a show jumping course.

Show jumping has gone through a metamorphosis in the past two decades. In the 1970s, the jumps were huge, but the tracks weren't technical. Today's riders and horses have figured out those big fences. And because jumps can be put only so high, what can a course designer do but make the track more challenging? The modern show jumping course is a test of a horse's athleticism, bravery, and rideability. For example, a course might require a rider to go from two fences that are related to fences where there is no relation of stride, on a twisting track, to a line of jumps that requires a short stride to a forward stride. The course designer may even put in half strides or change up the distances to test the horses' abilities, so the riders have to think about every approach.

One of the big misconceptions in show jumping is that the horse need not be schooled on the flat. Although many riders may want to concentrate on jumping their horses over ever-increasing heights and widths, the wise rider understands that flatwork is what divides the good from the great. In fact, a high-level jumper can usually execute a Third Level dressage test. This is because jumpers have to be adjustable longitudinally in order to lengthen their stride instantaneously—not three strides later, but when asked for by the rider. The horse must also be obedient and come back to her rider immediately. And she must let the rider regulate her gaits to make the short turns, bends, and changes of direction required in today's modern tracks. She also must be laterally flexible to stay supple and make those turns.

There are two distinct styles in the show jumping seat: the American style and the European style. Europeans tend to ride a little bit behind the motion of the horse and with more of a driving seat. Americans tend to ride in a two-point forward seat. The ultimate goal, however, is the same: to ride in balance with your horse. If that means being a little more upright and driving with your seat because that's what it takes to keep the horse balanced and forward, then that's what you do. If your horse is rolling along nicely, then you can stay in a lighter half seat. Whatever position you choose, you must follow the horse's motion over the fence.

Ultimately, form follows function: If you come up over the horse's shoulder, she might drop a rail. If you get left behind, she may catch a back rail. The length of stirrup for jumping is usually shorter compared with dressage and eventing. Because you want to get off the horse's back in the air, you need a more acute angle in your knee, hip, and ankle. However, adjust the stirrups to the length that makes you feel most comfortable.

This rider demonstrates the proper position for show jumping, with enough contact to give her a feel of her horse's mouth over the jump.

Show jumping riders will have a following contact, which allows them to keep a slight feel of the horse's mouth as she jumps. This gives the rider better influence over the horse as she lands and the ability to turn toward the next jump in balance and in control. If the rider chooses to make a turn in the air, she can do so with a slight opening rein. When hundredths of seconds count, every little bit helps.

Show Jumping Fences

At the higher levels, the design of show jumping fences has become an art form. But the types of jumps remain the same throughout all levels: verticals and spreads, which are either oxers or triple bars. Adjustability is key to show jumping. You should be able to gauge just how much pace and impulsion you need to get over each jump so that you don't have too much or too little energy on the other side. You must constantly evaluate your pace, your power, and how these relate to what you're jumping and what you're approaching.

Verticals

Vertical fences often won't have a ground line or object that helps place the horse at an ideal takeoff point. The fence is often set with planks rather than poles to add a higher degree of sophistication. But the vertical is essentially a single, plain fence. It requires the horse to rock back on her haunches and jump. The horse wants to jump in a big natural bascule, and a vertical is an up-and-down exercise without a lot of space in between. You can stand off a vertical a little bit but not so far that the horse risks flattening her jump. She still has to curl up and over it. As you ride toward the vertical, you need to factor in what's come before and what's coming next. If you're riding to just a single vertical on the course that's not related

Verticals like this are an up-and-down exercise without a lot of space between the horse's jump.

133

in stride to the other jumps, ideally you want a takeoff point that's a normal distance. You need to be sure that the takeoff point is far enough from the fence that the horse has enough time to rock back and bring her shoulders and front legs up and out of the way, but not so far that she risks flattening out at the top of her bascule and pulling the top rail.

Oxers

What makes oxers difficult is the spread element. Show jumping oxers are usually square rather than ramped like an ascending oxer, which helps the horse see what the spread is. Square oxers don't have this visual element, which adds a level of difficulty that tests the horse's ability to power over a fence. You must set this fence up similarly to the vertical but at the same time make sure the horse has enough power to jump across the fence. Ride your horse fairly strong and fairly close to the base of the oxer. The power is in the hindquarters. If they are not underneath the horse, she won't be able

A horse and rider approach an oxer in a show jumping course.

to access that power, so do not allow her to become hollow or strung out. The horse must be packaged between your leg and hand and feel as though you're winding a spring. As you get down to the base of the oxer, do not come forward with your body. Instead, wait, so that as the horse sits back to release the spring, your body gives her plenty of room to come back and to be free to lift up and over. In other words, you won't be in a very forward two-point; you will be in an upright and soft two-point—almost standing in the stirrups. If you are lying on her neck or leaning too far forward, she's going to have a much harder time getting her legs up and out of the way of the front rail. As she jumps, you will follow her up and over the fence naturally. In short, the horse must learn to set herself off of the oxer. And if you take off from too long a spot, the horse will not be able to get across the fence. She has to learn to power down, rock back, and fire up and across.

Water

A horse canters on a twelve-foot stride, and the biggest water spread is sixteen feet wide. Mad dashes can be overexcessive, but you have to pick up the pace so the horse has the energy she needs to bound over without expending a huge effort. Riding water all alone isn't very difficult; however, what often follows the water jump is an upright vertical fence, so if you land with your horse still going strong and you're desperately trying to reel her back in, you won't be able to jump the vertical.

Combinations

Show jumping combinations consist of two to three jumps. They are usually set on one- or two-stride relations. You must set up your approach correctly because you can do only so much adjusting in the one or two strides you have in between. If you jump into the combination wrong, there is little you can do to right it. The approach is critical. At the higher levels, designers won't set the combinations on

A rider schools her jumper over a combination.

exact twelve-foot strides; they will set them on either a short one stride to a long two strides or a short one stride to another short one stride. Balance and pace are critical. Again, think of winding your horse like a spring so that she has the compression and potential energy to see her through the combination. When a horse has to exert supreme efforts to get through combinations because of lack of help from her rider in the approach, she will lose confidence and begin to refuse. The importance of pace, approach, and position—the same factors involved in oxers and verticals—is magnified in combinations by the difficulty factor.

The Jump-Off

It's easy to get caught up in the heat of the moment and ride a jump-off as though it were Kentucky Derby time, forgetting about skill.

Turning the horse in the air like this is a time-saving technique for show jumpers.

This rider uses another time-saving technique: slicing across the jump at an angle toward the next jump.

Many people have the misconception that the jump-off is all about running hell for leather, which often results in disaster because there is always another jump ahead. Your horse has to slow down enough to balance and make the jump. You have to learn how much speed you can add and how much control you need to bring the horse back. Shaving time off the clock calls for craftiness as well as speed. To save time, a rider can cut a corner, turn in the air, or slice an angle across the jump, but not to the degree that he risks a jumping fault. The savvy jumper rider has the ability to ride the jump-off course and take more risks.

Plan your jump-off route during the course walk (see Have a Plan in chapter 12). As you walk the track, think of ways you can save time. For example, if you angle a wide square oxer, it gets wider and more difficult. However, you can angle a vertical or narrower oxer and save time there. Turning in the air is another option to consider, but think about where this is appropriate. If you turn too much, you can cause your horse to drop a hip or a shoulder and pull a rail. You may want to finish jumping the jump so that your horse has a chance to finish clean and make the turn. Turning through all of your jumps means you will jump them at an angle. But remember that you have to jump cleanly first—time is secondary!

Competition and the Advanced Rider

Becoming an advanced rider is a milestone in every rider's career, but it can also carry difficulties. As an advanced rider, you're more likely to be harder on yourself and on your horse. You may have also won competition after competition at your old level, but now you have to start at a much harder level and even compete with people who have been there a long while. Suddenly, competitions are no longer slam-dunks. Worst of all, you may even relapse into bad habits.

Have a Plan

The truth is, regardless of your level of expertise, change can be frightening. Fear can cause you to regress, and old habits that you thought you had kicked forever may begin to reappear. Perhaps old mental habits, such as self-doubt, forgetting things, or worrying about things, will come back; perhaps bad riding habits, such as pulling on the inside rein, will resurface.

This kind of fear is a natural aspect of moving out of your comfort zone and being uncomfortable again. When you're uncomfortable, your anxiety rises, and your old problems will come back just to remind you that you're not that accomplished. But there is hope. The thing to do is move up in very slow steps. In dressage, ride the last test in your former level and the first test in your new level to remind yourself that you can do it. Or in eventing, move up at a

A first-place winner takes a victory lap with her horse.

schooling or smaller show instead of at a big competition to avoid becoming overwhelmed. At your first time out, choose a familiar competition, an arena where you've shown before. Knowing where to park, knowing where the warm-up arenas are, remembering the way to the show office, and even something as simple as knowing what facilities are offered all reduce stress. And try not to move up to the next level on a totally different horse. In other words, make the new experience as much like the old experience as possible.

A good rule of thumb is to compete at a level below what you're practicing at home. In other words, compete at your top ability. This way, you won't be at your limit. Being at your limit and going through performance anxiety is too stressful a combination to be successful. You can't assume that you're going to be at your best when you're stressed out. If you pull back a bit and show at a level at which you're totally comfortable, the stress isn't going to cause you to regress as much.

Consider a bit of soul searching to make sure you're moving up for the right reasons. You may find that you feel pressured, either from outside sources or from yourself, to move up whether you're ready or not. Perhaps you've been at a lower level for too long, or maybe your friend is moving up and you feel left back. People also often buy trained horses and think they can ride at the horse's level. They know the horse can do it, so they think they can, too. In cases such as these, understand that it is OK to take your time. There is nothing to be gained from pressuring yourself only to fail miserably at the competition and risk destroying both your and your horse's confidence.

Advancing in Dressage

The transition from one level to the next shouldn't be difficult if you've established a solid foundation, paying close attention to the dressage training scale. The levels, after all, are designed to build on the tests in the previous levels. Therefore, if you've been doing a good job at your old level, putting in respectable performances and meeting the directives of each movement, the change to the next test or level should be a natural progression.

The tests at the lowest level, Training, allow judges to check that both rider and horse are heading in the right direction. This requires free forward movement in working gaits and paces, acceptance of the bit, and patterns that are somewhat clear—for instance, your circle should resemble a circle and begin and end at the same place. Since the lower levels are where riders and horses cut their teeth, judges are often more forgiving.

It's a whole different game in the next levels. For instance, in First Level, the paces (working trot and canter and medium and free walk) are exactly the same as those in Training Level but with the

A dressage rider competes at Fourth Level.

addition of lengthening of stride and transitions between lengthening and working paces. It has two movements, leg-yield and the stretching circle, but the level includes more difficult figures and transitions designed to be more demanding tests of a horse's balance. Mistakes that may not matter much at Training Level won't be so easily forgiven at First Level. Your horse must also show more impulsion. Study the directives at each level to understand what judges will expect from you and your horse.

Advancing in Eventing

Moving up in eventing is contingent on how you've competed at the lower levels. A common belief is that if a horse has competed successfully at his old level several times, he has probably gained enough experience, skills, and confidence to move up, but this means in all phases. Eventing used to be all about cross-country, and competitions were won and lost on this phase. This is no longer true; today, all three phases are equally important. Mess up dressage, and you'll have

A young rider competes in cross-country.

to really shine at the next two phases to place. Therefore, don't put all your faith in your horse's ability to compete at the higher level simply because his cross-country is exemplary.

Dressage can be difficult for a lot of event horses because they are very fit; their entire musculature is different from that of dressage horses, so it's hard to make them relaxed and supple. They often get tense and excited because they want to run cross-country. This tension can carry over into the stadium, where you have to be accurate to jump modern stadium courses. For example, narrow (or skinny) fences are now the norm in many events. Narrow fences require greater accuracy because the face of the jump is slight, so it's easier for the horse to run out.

It's understandable to want to test your mettle on harder, more complicated cross-country jumps at home. But you can make things worse by trying to school these difficult jumps. You may end up overfacing your horse and creating a confidence problem. However, you can still school the concept by riding over combinations and jumps encountered at higher levels, at very low settings.

Advancing in Hunters

In hunters, style and technique count; it's not just about clearing the obstacle. Moving up very much depends on the inherent quality and ability of the horse. Because hunters are judged subjectively on such criteria as style of jumping, movement, and overall quality, they can be forever stuck at the lower levels if they don't have what it takes to advance. In other words, if a horse is limited in his scope, soundness, and style at two feet, six inches to three feet, there's no point in moving on.

Moving up also depends on your desire and ambition. The lower levels of hunters, especially on the county or regional circuits, are huge. Many riders, particularly adult amateurs, can spend their entire show career showing at the two feet, six inches to three feet–level, winning all kinds of awards. This is in part because show

Make sure your hunter is jumping in good style before moving up to bigger fences. Notice that this horse's knees aren't even.

management realizes that many, many adults have to squeeze riding time into busy lives. They don't have the time or motivation to move up to bigger heights.

The baby green division is where most hunters start. Here, the jumps are as low as two feet, three inches, and minor faults such as playing in the corners, maybe skipping a lead change, are often forgiven. Only when the young horse knows its job is it moved up to pre-green or the proper division for the horse's owner (such as junior hunters or amateur adult hunters).

A green horse that is ready to advance is one that doesn't rush through the lines. The green horse must be able to carry himself on a steady, consistent twelve-foot stride to make the prescribed counts (strides) in a line. He should not land after the first jump in a line, take a bead on the second element, elevate his head, and gallop off to the next jump to make the counts. Some horses don't have a naturally long step, which means they can never graduate to the bigger fences and tougher courses. A horse is also ready to move up if he can perform flying lead changes cleanly, because if you miss a flying lead change in hunters, you're out. And finally, the horse's jumping style should stay impressive as the fences get bigger and stouter. If a green horse begins to jump out over his front end or twist in the air, he's telling the rider that he's struggling; he is no longer thinking about his body position but is just aiming to get from one side of the jump to the other.

Advancing in Show Jumping

The bigger, the better seems to be the motto in show jumping; and of course, that's where the top prize money often is, too. However, speed and the ability to jump big fences aren't exactly the best gauge for advancement. Modern courses demand more from a horse and rider, and skills gained during your flatwork will stand you in good stead as you advance through the various divisions. A good rule of thumb is to consider advancing when both you and your horse are consistently jumping clear rounds without riding errors. For instance, if you can go clear nine times in a row but you still have distance problems or rideability issues, wait until you've worked out these problems before moving up. If you can jump around a course clearly and comfortably within the time and make it look like an equitation round, these are good indicators that both you and your horse are ready to advance.

However, jumpers frequently (even at the highest levels) move up and down. So move up, test the water, and then move back down

A show jumper and rider clear a fence. When you're successful at completing courses cleanly, it's time to move up.

again. Don't fall into the trap of thinking that once you're up, you
have to stay there forever. If you need to practice a skill or technique
for yourself or your horse, you can drop down a level so that the
degree of difficulty of the course is not your prime focus. This will
allow you to concentrate on the skill, and you'll gain more confidence and success as a result.

Getting Ready for a Competition

Few of us have the ready cash to hire a competition groom, so in most cases the rider does all the work of preparing for a competition. This can create a heavy workload, which on top of the pressure of perfecting your riding technique makes the competition experience even more stressful. There are several ways around this; early preparation and good planning are the keys.

Prep Yourself

Before you send in your first entry form, clear up a few more tasks at home. First, go over your equipment and check for needed repairs. Examine your tack and make sure the stitching is sound and safe, especially (for obvious safety reasons) your stirrup leathers, girth, and reins. Look at your horse's competition equipment, and check for broken buckles or torn Velcro. Now is also a good time to make an appointment with your saddler to adjust or reflock your saddle, if needed. If you're going to a three-day event, change the batteries in your stopwatch.

Check all your competition clothes, including your body protector and helmet, and make sure they are up to scratch. Make sure that everything still fits and your boots are in good shape.

Make sure your medical card is up to date if you are an eventer. A medical card is required at all levels of recognized events. Some

A rider grooms her horse's tail in preparation for a competition.

Familiarity helps keep nerves at bay, so choose a known venue when moving up.

nonrecognized events are requiring them as well. The medical card lists your personal information, including blood type, insurance information, previous injuries, and emergency contacts. The card slips inside a plastic sleeve that can be wrapped around your arm with an elastic-and-Velcro sleeve.

Replace that latest best-seller on your bedside table with your discipline's rulebook or dressage test booklet. Review the rulebook until you know it well. There's no point in getting to a competition only to be disqualified because you didn't know a simple rule or rule change. And learn your dressage test backward and forward. For some championships and event competitions, it has to be memorized. Know your

Organization will help streamline preparation. Make it permanent by storing competition equipment in boxes, such as this tack box.

test so well that you won't be worried about whether you should turn left or right and can concentrate on making your shoulder-in or medium trot the best it can be.

Prep Your Equipment

Next, organize your equipment. Don't make the mistake of organizing your gear at the last minute. If you are running around the night before trying to trace where you left your white dressage pad or worrying about whether you have the right bridle, you are going to be focused on organization and not on your ride. Therefore, make your organization permanent. Purchase several large plastic boxes with lids, and put all the necessary equipment for each type of competition or phase in its own box. Compile an after-competition box with such items as a sweat sheet, leg wraps, and liniment for your horse's legs. Include a first-aid kit containing wound cream, gauze bandages, and a thermometer. Keep all your competition clothing together. Store the clothing as separate outfits in garment bags. In each bag, keep all the clothes you'll wear for each competition or phase. Store your helmets or hats in boxes and your show boots (if you have them) with spurs in a boot bag, and store any miscellaneous gear, such as hairnets and pins, in another small box alongside your clothes.

If you're eventing, you'll need several changes of clothes: beige or white breeches, black jacket, white shirt, stock tie, and stock pin for the dressage in one bag; helmet cover, breeches, and shirt for the cross-country in another bag; white shirt, tie, jacket, breeches, and helmet cover for the show jumping phase in another bag.

Keep your boxes in your trailer or all in one place so everything is ready to go when the day comes. And be disciplined. When you come back from the competition, clean everything and put each item back in its box or bag, ready for the next competition. If you want to be superorganized, keep a checklist and mark each entry as you return the item to the box.

In addition to preparing the horse's tack, competitors must organize their apparel.

Prep Your Horse: A Braiding Primer

Braiding your horse for a competition shows respect for the judge and the competition. It is also a way of telling the judge that you have paid attention to every detail and have gone the extra mile to make your horse look as good as possible.

Here is a list of equipment you are likely to need for braiding:

- braid aid (if desired)
- braiding product (if desired)
- hair clip or clothes pin
- pulling comb
- pull-through or latch hook
- seam ripper to remove the yarn
- small scissors (sewing scissors with tiny, pointed blades work best)
- sponge and bucket to wet the mane (if desired)
- step stool
- yarn to match the color of the mane (cut to length by winding around thumb and elbow, then cut top and bottom of the "loop" to make the pieces)

Step One: Mane Preparation. It's always a good idea to keep your horse's mane pulled so you don't have to do a massive grooming job on your horse right before a show. If that's not possible, try to shorten the mane to length—about six inches—about a week before the show. Shampoo the mane a few days before you braid it, but do not use conditioner or coat polish; if you do, the yarn will just slip out of the mane.

Step Two: Making Braids. Assemble your equipment and secure your horse. Thread a hank of yarn (cut to about ten to twelve inches) through your belt loop or, if your horse doesn't mind, through the top ring of her halter. Begin by either spraying water or a braiding product onto the mane. To make the braids equal in thickness, use a braid aid or a comb, and section off a small ponytail of mane.

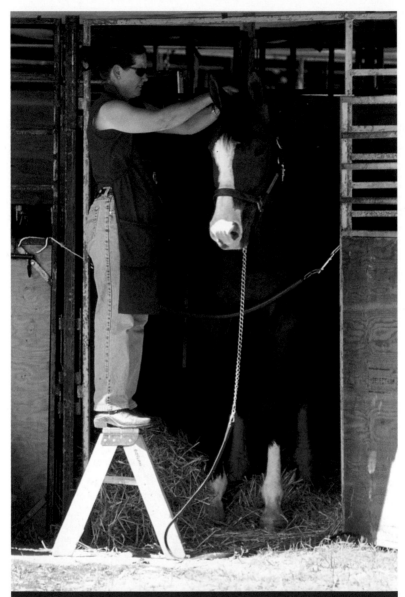

The proper equipment is essential for braiding. This step stool makes the task easier.

Make sure that the parting is very straight. Once you've made your partings, use a clothespin or hair clip to hold the rest of the mane out of the way.

Grasp the ponytail and divide it into three sections. Always start braiding with the same strand for every braid. For instance, if you start with the right strand of your first ponytail, begin braiding all other ponytails with the right strand. This makes the braids' appearance more uniform. As you braid the ponytail, clamp a thumb in the middle of each turning to keep the pressure of the braid tight and even.

When you are halfway down the braid, hold the middle of the braid with one thumb, and place a piece of yarn folded in half underneath your thumb. Continue braiding, but this time incorporate the yarn pieces into the right and left strands of the braid. Remember to keep the pressure up. When you can't braid any longer, clamp off the braid with your thumb and forefinger. Take the two tails of the yarn and wind them around the end twice and pass them through to make a knot. Tie the braid off again. You should have a tight braid that lies flat with about five inches of yarn hanging down. Braid the rest of the mane in the same way.

Step Three: Tying Off. Using your pull-through, begin pulling up the braids. Insert the pull-through into the center of the braid from the top to the base of the crest. Insert the yarn through the loop of the pull-through, and bring the yarn back up through the top of the braid. Release the yarn and, with your hand, gently pull the yarn ends so that the knotted end of the braid is hidden in the base of the braid. Make sure that none of the prickly bits are sticking out of the top. Press the braid down flat. Cross the yarn ends behind the braid and knot it. Bring the pieces around to the front of the braid, knot it in the middle of the braid, and clip off the ends of the yarn.

If you like, before you tie off the knot, you can push the braid up so that a little bobble of braid extends above the neck. Tie the knot just under this bobble. The trick is to keep all the bobbles even as you pull the other braids up. This type of braiding is more commonly seen

A beautifully braided mane like this tells the judge that you've paid attention to every detail and that you respect your sport.

in the dressage world. Hunter braids usually lie flat against the neck. Hunters are shown with braids on the right side of the neck only. This is an old tradition that hails from the hunting fields. Riders mount on the left so braids must be on the right to avoid getting the hunting garb tangled in the braids. Dressage horses can be braided either right or left, as the rider chooses.

You can repeat the same braiding process on the forelock, or if you're feeling creative, you can French-braid the forelock. Begin by sectioning the top of the forelock into two strands. Start braiding and gather up the third strand from each side of the forelock as you go down the forehead. As you reach the dangling end of the forelock, return to braiding normally. Tie the knot off, pull it through the forelock, and tie it off as you did with the mane. Another nice finish is to forgo tying off the braid. Instead, pull the braid up through the forelock, and bring the tail of the braid completely through. Fish that end back through the braid with your pull-through (from the bottom of the braid). Continue to pull the tail through the braid until the tail end is tucked completely under the braid.

On the Day of the Show

"Time waits for no man." A simple phrase, and perhaps a cliché, but true nonetheless, so on the day of a show, give yourself plenty of time. Once you know your times for each class or phase, sit down and make a schedule. Plan sensibly: do as many chores the day before as you can. If you're competing the same day you travel, provide extra time for loading mishaps, leave your stable before the traffic starts, and fill your truck with gasoline the night before. Figure in an extra hour for emergencies. Then you'll have extra time, and you won't be rushed. Estimate your arrival time, and give yourself a block of time to walk the course, warm up, and get dressed. If you're confident that you have enough time to accomplish each task, you'll be able to concentrate on your plan of action instead of obsessing about rushing to warm up your horse.

Walking the Course

At a one-day event, the course isn't as long as it is at a three-day competition, and you may not have enough time to walk it more than once. A three-day is another matter. Plan to walk the course many times to make certain you are prepared. Take note of every tree you line up with, every route you take for every fence. If your horse doesn't go very well or if you aren't feeling very confident, you'll know for sure what the alternative route is. Routes are important

A rider considers the alternatives at this water jump.

when you're walking the course. Know the direct route, and be aware of all the alternatives so if you have a stop you'll know the route to take. If there is no alternative, decide what you'll do if you have a stop.

It's important, at whatever level you are riding, that you jump the fence in the correct place, either right in the middle for a straight-forward fence or the right line for a corner. Be aware of the best ground conditions, and know where the boggy patches are.

Riders share their knowledge, and the best way they can do that is while walking the course. Don't be shy about going up to seasoned riders and asking if you can walk along with them. At some events, the organizers will announce a course walk with a particular rider at a particular time. The rider will meet a group of people, and they'll all walk the course together.

Hunter riders don't walk a course; instead, they study the course map posted at the back gate. Look at the measurements on the course diagram. Since strides at a show are measured in twelve-foot increments, the course designer will usually (always at larger shows) write down how he or she measured the lines when the course was initially set. So a line measured at seventy-two feet will ride in five strides (twelve feet is used up with six feet for landing in a line and six feet for taking off out over the last element). Usually, only a few different courses are used throughout the day, so by watching a few rounds, even in divisions other than your own, you can see how the course rides and what the strides are like. In other words, the wise hunter rider watches and learns how to ride the course.

Walking a course is critical to the jumper rider. In fact, you will be at a serious disadvantage in a major class if you don't walk it. A diagram of the course will be posted, but it will not specify the distances between the jumps that are related; this is something you will discover yourself.

To work out the distances between your jumps, you must stride it out. To do this, you must first know the length of your own stride, which is individual to you. Figure out your personal stride by putting a tape measure on the ground and walking out in a large, but not exaggerated, stride. Measure between the spaces from toe to toe; a normal stride is about three feet. So, when walking the course,

Two competitors walk the course together to check the ground conditions and to strategize their individual rides.

stand with your back on the landing side of the jump, in the middle of the fence, and take one stride out (to allow for the horse to land), then stride out in multiples of four (which would be one average canter length). Remember to walk the way you want to ride it; in corners and curves, if that's your plan.

When walking the course, you must take several things into consideration. Does the ring have terrain, and if so, how does it relate to the jumps? What are the distances between the fences that are related? Are they on a straight line to one another or on a bend?

Another common design in jumper courses is distances on the half stride, so, for instance, fence three to four is 6½ strides. You must consider the jumps (whether they are oxers or verticals) and how your own horse goes. There is no absolute answer to this type of course question; although a one stride is always a one stride, it may require you to ride it steady or normal or forward.

You must also take into account the relationship of a jump that requires a forward ride (like the water jump) to the next fence. Harder courses will have the water followed by a relatively short distance (six or seven strides) to another jump, often a vertical, where the rider has to be able to immediately get the horse back after making a forward, stretching effort over the water and to collect and reengage to then jump the vertical with control and cleanly.

Combinations, either one stride or two strides, can be a double combination (two jumps) or a triple combination (three jumps). During your walk, see if the strides are normal, steady, long, or a combination of the three—for instance, a normal two stride followed by a steady one stride. And what are the fence types, verticals or spreads (oxers), and what is their relationship to one another? Are you jumping into the combination over an oxer and then one stride to a vertical and then out over an oxer? Or is it vertical to vertical to a huge, square oxer?

Next, think about how the jumps are constructed, including elements of trickery. For instance, there might be bright rails up high with a dark black plank down low that will draw the horse's eye down and possibly make him think he is jumping into a hole. The jump may be constructed all of poles, or the top element may be a plank. Although the cups are fairly shallow to begin with, planks are usually set on an absolutely flat cup and come down with the lightest touch.

You also need to know the time allowed, which will be posted on the course diagram. Plotting it against the course will help you decide if the allowed time will be tight, normal, or generous. If you feel it is tight, try to work out some track options that will make the

50° 46' N

6° 6' E

This fence is constructed of planks set in shallow cups that can easily be knocked down with the slightest rap.

time allowed more generous and give you more time riding some of the tougher sections of the course. Think, as you walk the course, where you can save yourself time. Or perhaps you will decide you'll have to ride aggressively throughout the entire course to stay within the time allowed.

These are some of the basic thoughts that go into planning your ride. Going later in the order allows you to watch earlier rides and make minor adjustments. However, some riders swear by walking the course, making the best plan they can for their horses, and then not considering (or watching) earlier rides. The one time you might want to consider other results is when their times in general are playing out differently than you anticipated.

Warming Up

The bigger shows usually offer two warm-up arenas: one to lunge in, and one to ride in. Smaller shows, where space is an issue, normally provide one arena with the center reserved for lunging. This can be tricky because the riders on the rail must watch out for those horses lunging. Someone invariably tries to get between the horse and the handler who's lunging. You have to realize that there's not a lot of control with the horse on the end of the lunge line—he can buck or kick out, so you've got to give him a little bit of room, at least a horse's length.

Jumping

For all jumping disciplines, make sure your horse is well warmed up before you start to jump; do lots of canter work and transitions, lots of bending, turning right and left in canter and in trot so you'll know your horse is warmed up in his back. Once you've done this for about twenty to thirty minutes, depending on your horse, jump a cross rail a couple of times, then add a vertical, and finish over an oxer. Remember that the goal is not to school your horse but to get him thinking about the task at hand. Good riders do not overjump

A show jumping competitor and her horse warm up before their class.

their horses in the warm-up. It is warm-up, not training. Some flat-work can be done hours before the class, especially when there is an afternoon class. This allows the horse to get out and stay loose.

A competitor and coach watch other riders navigate a show jumping course to make minor adjustments.

Cross-Country

The main goals of cross-country warm-up are to get your horse going forward and to make sure he is alert and concentrating. In a one-day event, you may do your stadium jumping first, and you won't have a lot of time before you're off on your cross-country. Your horse won't have enough time to switch off. So go back to your trailer, change into your cross-country gear, then get back on, have a spin around the warm-up ring, jump the practice jump four or five times, and head out to the course.

A dressage horse and rider warm up before a competition.

Dressage

For dressage, get out into the warm-up arena early to bring your horse's energy level down, about an hour before, particularly if you want to lunge and ride. But some horses need more time and some need less; all riders should know what their horse requires. If your horse hasn't been to a lot of shows, he's going to be more excitable. If he's an old campaigner, he might not need much calming. Also, remember that the show is not the place to train your horse. If your horse doesn't know his work, you're not going to teach him in the warm-up arena. So treat the warm-up as a time to loosen your horse's muscles, sharpen his focus, and get ready to work.

Rules of the Warm-Up Arena

Here is a list of rules to follow when riding in the warm-up arena:

- Pass left hand to left hand. However, the best thing you can do is keep your head up. There may be a rider who needs some extra room and who may not be able to pass on the left side, or perhaps there might be a rider on a really green horse. If you keep your head up and you're making eye contact with a rider, you can tell which way the traffic is moving.
- Someone may call out "rail, please" in an effort to get you to give way. You don't have to move out of the way, but that person may be in trouble and need the space, so respect the request. Always give way to the inexperienced person, the young horse, or a child.
- Horses at the slower gait have the right-of-way on the rail. Just as on the freeway, faster drivers pull out onto the far lane and pass. The slower horse stays on the rail and keeps his position. However, rail riders should to be aware of people attempting to pass and avoid swinging out into the faster traffic.
- If you see someone working a pattern in the center of the arena, show consideration. Don't ride into his pattern.

- At jumping competitions, a vertical and an oxer are usually provided by the organizer. Warm-up arenas with jumps can be a free-for-all, but using etiquette can make things go more smoothly. Ask the other riders if they mind if you adjust the jump height, but then put it back the way you found it. Have a groundsperson replace the rail if you drop it. Don't cut across riders' tracks, and make sure you know who is going next. The key is to be friendly and communicate with the other riders.
- Don't be intimidated by trainers and their riders. You have just as much right to warm up your horse as any other rider does. Expect that a bigger trainer may try to push you around or try to bully. Just hold your space, say "excuse me," and go on with your warm-up.

After the warm-up, this horse is able to focus on the task at hand: jumping the course.

Competition Psychology

Nerves can affect riders at all levels, particularly when a new challenge is involved. Suddenly the dressage test seems too difficult or the size and spread of the fences seem to grow bigger in your imagination. Often, on the morning of the show you wonder why you are competing at all. But as soon as you get on the horse you realize why: because competition is really fun and a good way to stretch yourself as a rider. There is a lot to think about, but try to stay calm and concentrate on keeping your horse relaxed. You just have to be determined that you are going to stay relaxed and focused. Find out what works for you and keeps you calm. You may find that listening to CDs or talking with friends does it for you. Some riders find the routine of readying their horses calming; others find it winds them up and would rather hire a groom for the day or ask a friend to help so they can concentrate fully on their strategies. The more competitions you participate in, the more you'll discover about handling inevitable nerves.

Learn from Past Experiences

If you have a disappointing competition, rather than giving it all up, try to turn it into a learning experience. Analyze what went wrong, and think of ways you can make it better. Keep a journal of what happened so you have something useful to refer to for later compe-

Before the show, a rider focuses on staying calm and preparing her horse for the competition.

titions. You might write, "I worked Dandy for half an hour before the dressage, which was too much, so he went flat during the test." Include suggestions; perhaps, "Suggest 20 minutes warm-up in dressage next time." And then, before the next competition, make sure you refer to your notes from the previous competition. Writing everything down forms a picture of what works and what doesn't work. Then play with different ideas of what to do. Perhaps you've written, "In cross-country, I had a stop at the ditch, it was a spooky

A rider takes notes. Record notes from your recent competition in a journal for future reference.

downhill ditch, he seems to jump everything on the flat. OK. So let's practice going downhill to a ditch." Find a course with a ditch downhill with a bit of a drop down to it and train your horse. Eventually, through your journal, you'll have a clear picture of your successes and how you got the best results, as well as a plan of action for solving problems. Don't forget to note what worked for you in your competition. It's always best to end your thoughts on a positive note.

Employ a Calming Technique

Neurofeedback (NFB) is an up-and-coming technique that has sports psychologists taking notice. Neurofeedback psychologists say that athletes focus best when they generate strong brain waves in the twelve-to-fifteen-hertz range (a measurement of how fast the brain is cycling). Some people have to calm down to hit this target range; others have to get more active and revved up. If you are generating brain waves in higher ranges, you'll often feel wound up. If you're generating brain waves in lower ranges, you'll feel spacey. So you have to find a way to reach the optimal range. The simplest way is by deep belly breathing, similar to yogic breathing. Put one hand on your chest and one hand on your stomach, and take a deep breath. The hand on your stomach should move more than the hand on your chest. Inhale for a count of four, exhale for a count of four, and repeat. Another element of the technique is maintaining a level eye gaze. A focused gaze and deep breathing will bring both the keyed-up athlete and the flat athlete to the ideal range.

Advanced English riding is more than just learning how to keep your heels down or getting the hang of the posting trot. Once you understand the basics, your choices are endless. You can choose to specialize in one discipline, such as dressage, or sample a little of what each one has to offer. You can advance in your choice, whether by jumping bigger fences or tackling more intricate combinations, trickier lateral work, or more difficult dressage patterns. The most

A rider receives a championship ribbon. Keep riding, keep learning, and you'll continue to improve throughout your riding career.

important thing to understand about advanced riding is that you will never complete your riding education. English riding is very complex, and although you can learn something new every time you ride, you can never learn everything. Even top Olympic athletes continue to take lessons. Keeping an open mind and being a lifelong student will advance your skills in a positive and fulfilling way.

Resources

American Association of Equine
Practitioners (AAEP)
4075 Iron Works Parkway
Lexington, Kentucky 40511
859-233-0147
http://www.aaep.org
Straight from the source:
"The American Association of
Equine Practitioners (AAEP)
is the world's largest professional association of equine veteri-
narians. The AAEP's mission is
to improve the health and welfare of the horse, to further the
professional development of its
members, and to provide
resources and leadership for the
benefit of the equine industry."

American Horse Council (AHC)
1616 H Street NW, 7th Floor
Washington, DC 20006
202-296-4031
http://www.horsecouncil.org
Straight from the source:
"As the national trade association representing the horse industry in Washington, D.C., the
American Horse Council works
daily to represent your equine
interests and investments.
Organized in 1969, the AHC has
been promoting and protecting
the industry by communicating
with Congress, federal agencies,
the media and the industry itself
on behalf of all horse related
interests each and every day."

American Society for the
Prevention of Cruelty to Animals
(ASPCA)
424 E. 92nd Street
New York, New York
10128-6804
212-876-7700
http://www.aspca.org
Straight from the source:
"The ASPCA, the first humane
society in North America and,
today, one of the largest humane
societies in the world, was founded by Henry Bergh and incorporated in 1866 by a special act of
the New York State legislature.
The mission of the ASPCA, as
stated by Henry Bergh in 1866,
is 'to provide effective means
for the prevention of cruelty to
animals throughout the United
States.'"

The Communication Alliance
to Network Thoroughbred
Ex-Racehorses (CANTER)
2760 East Lansing Drive, Suite 5
East Lansing, Michigan 48823
517-351-0014
http://www.canterusa.org
Straight from the source:
"A unique affiliation of 501(c)(3)
nonprofit organizations dedicated
to providing retiring racehorses
with opportunities for new
careers after the finish line."

The Humane Society of the
United States (HSUS)
2100 L Street NW
Washington, DC 20037
202-452-1100
http://www.hsus.org
From the source:
"HSUS has worked since 1954
to promote the protection of all
animals. With nearly ten million
members and constituents, the
HSUS is the nation's largest and
most powerful animal protection
organization, working in the
United States and abroad to
defend the interests of animals.
We celebrate the human-animal
bond, and we fight animal cruelty
and abuse in all of its forms."

Intercollegiate Dressage
Association (IDA)
Johnson & Wales University
29 Frances Street
Rehoboth, Massachusetts 02769
508-252-3027
http://www.teamdressage.com
Straight from the source:
"The mission of IDA is to introduce students to the equestrian
discipline of dressage and to
foster continued development,
understanding and appreciation
in the art of dressage through
organized student competitions
and educational opportunities."

Intercollegiate Horse Show
Association (IHSA)
http://www.ihsainc.com
Straight from the source:

"The association was founded
on the principle that any college
student should be able to participate in horse shows regardless of
his or her financial status or riding
level. Emphasis is on learning,
sportsmanship, and fun. Competition plays a role but the students'
enthusiasm and team spirit are the
major factors. The objective of
IHSA competition is to offer the
opportunity to riders in their first
years of riding as well as to students with show experience.
Eliminating the expense of ship-
ping or even owning horses puts
IHSA competitions within reach of
many who would otherwise miss
the equestrian experience."

International Federation for
Equestrian Sports (FEI)
Avenue Mon Repos 24
1005 Lausanne
Switzerland
+44 21 310 47 47
http://www.horsesport.org
Straight from the source:
"The primary mission of the
FEI is to advance the orderly
growth of equestrian sport
world-wide by promoting, regu-
lating and administering humane
and sportsmanlike international
competition in the traditional
equestrian disciplines and by
helping them to evolve in ways
that enhance their attractiveness
both for the participants and
the public, while respecting
and furthering the ideals and

principles of horsemanship. The FEI is based on the principle of equality and mutual respect between all National Federations, without prejudice to race, color, religion or internal politics."

The International Hunter Futurity
PO Box 13244
Lexington, Kentucky
40583-3244
859-879-3600
http://www.inthf.org
Straight from the source:
"The International Hunter Futurity, a competition for young hunters, has emerged as a method of promoting the hunter to a position of prominence in the world of horse sports."

The International Side Saddle Organization
PO Box 57
Vineland, New Jersey
08362-0057
856-696-8949
http://www.sidesaddle.com
Straight from the source:
"The International Side Saddle Organization is one of the world's oldest formal groups devoted to the promotion and preservation of the fine art of riding aside. We strive to provide you with information, resources and educate you about riding aside, whether you are a rider, instructor, or simply interested in knowing more about side saddle."

Kentucky Horse Park
4089 Iron Works Parkway
Lexington, Kentucky 40511
859-233-4303
http://www.kyhorsepark.com
Straight from the source:
"The Kentucky Horse Park is an equine themed park and competition facility dedicated to man's relationship with the horse. Set on more than 1,200 acres in the heart of Kentucky's famous Bluegrass region, the park is THE place to get close to horses! Home to approximately 50 different breeds, large and small, the park introduces you to the world of the horse."

Master Saddlers Association
2698 Jennings Chapel Road
Woodbine, Maryland 21797
301-570-3100
http://www.mastersaddlers.com
Straight from the source:
"The Master Saddlers Association was established in order to provide education for the general horse riding and owning public and for the training, certification and continuing education of saddle fitters. In this way, the needs of the horse owner, rider and, most importantly, the horses themselves can be fully catered to in regards to the vital issue of saddle fit."

Masters of Foxhounds
Association of North America
(MFHA)
PO Box 363
Millwood, Virginia 22646
540-955-5680
http://www.mfha.com
Straight from the source:
"The Masters of Foxhounds
Association of America is the
governing body of organized fox,
coyote and drag hunting in the
United States of America and
Canada."

The National Hunter & Jumper
Association, Inc.
7 Steep Hollow Lane
Cos Cob, Connecticut 06807
(June through December)
7414 NW 45th Lane
Ocala, Florida 34482 (January
through May)
http://www.nhja.org
Straight from the source:
"The object of the National
Hunter & Jumper Association is
to deal with issues and concerns
related to the showing of hunters
and jumpers through all levels of
competition from the 'grassroots'
entry level exhibitor to the
Olympic rider."

North American Riding for the
Handicapped Association, Inc.
(NARHA)
PO Box 33150
Denver, Colorado 80233
800-369-7433
http://www.narha.org

Straight from the source:
"NARHA is a national non-
profit organization that promotes
the benefit of the horse for indi-
viduals with physical, emotional
and learning disabilities. For indi-
viduals with disabilities, equine-
assisted activities have been
shown to improve muscle tone,
balance, posture, coordination,
motor development as well as
emotional well-being."

United States Dressage
Federation (USDF)
4051 Iron Works Parkway
Lexington, Kentucky 40511
859-971-2277
http://www.usdf.org
Straight from the source: "USDF
was established for the purpose
of promoting and encouraging a
high standard of accomplishment
in dressage throughout the
United States, primarily through
educational programs."

United States Equestrian
Federation, Inc. (USEF)
4047 Iron Works Parkway
Lexington, Kentucky 40511
859-258-2472
http://www.usef.org
Straight from the source: "The
vision of United States Equestrian
Federation is to provide leadership for equestrian sport in the
United States of America, promoting the pursuit of excellence
from the grass roots to the
Olympic Games, based on a

foundation of fair, safe competition and the welfare of its human and equine athletes, and embracing this vision, to be the best national equestrian federation in the world."

United States Equestrian Team Foundation (USET)
1040 Pottersville Road
PO Box 355
Gladstone, New Jersey 07934-9955
908-234-1251
http://www.uset.com
Straight from the source: "The United States Equestrian Team Foundation supports equestrian athletes, promotes international excellence, and builds for the future of equestrian sports. The eight High Performance equestrian disciplines supported by the United States Equestrian Team Foundation are dressage, driving, endurance, eventing, para-equestrian, reining, show jumping and vaulting."

United States Eventing Association, Inc. (USEA)
525 Old Waterford Road NW
Leesburg, Virginia 20176
703-779-0550
http://www.useventing.com
Straight from the source: "The USEA sanctions more than 280 competitions each year all across the United States. More than 40,000 riders compete annually in these events. Eventing competi-

tions present a variety of competition levels from Novice through Advanced, and the added geographic diversity of the sport truly offers competitive opportunities for horse enthusiasts of every age, skill-level and region in the U.S."

United States Hunter Jumper Association (USHJA)
4047 Iron Works Parkway
Lexington, Kentucky 40511
859-258-9033
http://www.ushja.org
Straight from the source: "The USHJA is committed to advancing and representing the hunter and jumper disciplines by fostering an educated community of equestrians that promotes the welfare of the horse and fairness in competition."

Glossary

above the bit: A position in which the horse raises his neck so that the mouth is higher than the rider's hand, resulting in little control; the back is also hollow. Considered an evasion.

aids: Communication to horse by rider using hands, seat, and leg. Artificial aids include use of whip and spurs.

automatic release: The contact with the horse's mouth is held over fences. The rider must follow the contact.

bank: A cross-country fence that asks the horse to jump up and off of an element.

behind the bit: A position in which the horse evades the rider's contact by dropping his nose behind the vertical position.

bounce: Jump requiring a horse to jump over a fence and then directly over another without taking a stride in between. Also called an in and out.

cavalletti: Italian for "little jump," today's cavalletti is a variety of poles used to overcome problems in jumping and flatwork.

change of rein: Change from one direction to another, for example, the right rein to the left rein.

coffin: The rail, ditch, rail combination fence in cross-country.

collection: Increased bend of the hind legs to carry more weight in the haunches.

connection: A state in which the energy from the horse's hind legs travels through the body to the forehand and "connects" to the rider's hand; the momentum from the hind legs can be channeled in a usable way.

contact: The horse moves forward to the bit freely.

core muscles: Muscles in the trunk (abdomen, back, and pelvis) of the body that are responsible for posture.

corner: A cross-country fence that requires the horse and rider to jump the extreme end of the fence.

crest release: Reins are relinquished over the fence by placing the hands halfway up the horse's crest, as opposed to an automatic release.

derby bank: A substantial bank that requires the horse and rider to canter up, jump an obstacle on the top, and then jump or ride down the opposite side of the bank.

diagonal aid: An aid that uses the rider's inside leg to outside rein. Helps balance the horse and is used while bending and straightening.

drop: A cross-country fence that requires the horse to jump off of it rather than over it.

extended: Pace that builds from a collected gait. Requires increased impulsion and has a larger reach and stretch of the topline than the medium pace.

fifteen-meter circle: Circle that is fifteen meters in circumference. In a standard dressage arena, this circle would touch the farthest quarter line.

figure: Pattern used in flatwork.

figure-eight noseband: Noseband that has a long figure-eight setup. The bottom piece is fastened below the snaffle bit. Gives increased control over the horse's jaw. Commonly found in eventing and show jumping.

flash noseband: Noseband that consists of two pieces—the standard noseband and the flash attachment, which hangs from the noseband and is fastened below the snaffle bit. Commonly found in dressage.

flying change: Canter lead is changed within the stride.

forward, downward stretch: The horse is allowed to stretch the head and neck down toward the ground, thereby lifting and strengthening the topline muscles. Also a check to prove that the horse has been working correctly on the bit.

free walk on a long rein: Movement in dressage in which the horse stretches down on a long rein, demonstrating a loose, swinging back and free rhythmic walk.

full bridge: A rein position used in galloping; the two opposite reins are stretched across the horse's neck to give the rider added control and stability.

gallops: Areas specifically set aside for galloping. Must have good footing and visibility.

gridwork: Also called gymnastic jumping, grids improve technique and style over fences.

half bridge: A rein position used in galloping in which a single rein is stretched across the horse's neck to give the rider control and stability.

half halt: Aid that works to slow the front end of the horse while the hind legs continue to move forward, causing the horse to balance on the haunches.

half pass: A two-track movement in which the horse is bent in the direction of travel.

hand gallop: A longer-stride canter with increased speed (375 to 450 mpm). The horse is still controllable, or in hand.

impulsion: Pushing power of the hind legs in trot and canter.

in and out: A jump requiring the horse to jump over a fence and then directly over another without taking a stride in between. Also called a bounce.

independent position: Riding position that doesn't rely on the horse for balance or security.

jump-off: The final in show jumping against the clock on a shortened, often higher course, to determine the winner.

lateral work: Sideways exercises that increase engagement and loosen the horse's shoulders and back.

leg yield: Suppling exercise in which the horse crosses and uncrosses his legs as his travels. Horse is slightly bent away from direction of movement.

lengthening: Pace developed from a working gait. The frame and stride of the horse lengthens.

looseness: Relaxation of the horse and the acceptance of the rider's aids. The horse moves correctly at the tempo set by the rider.

medium pace: Pace that builds from a collected gait. Requires increased impulsion from the hind legs and a bigger stride.

meters per minute (mpm): The number of meters the horse covers in one minute. Used primarily in eventing to denote the speed needed to complete the cross-country phase. For example, Preliminary Level is set at 520 mpm.

neurofeedback (NFB): Modern psychological technique that teaches people to adjust their brain waves.

on the bit: A functional position in which the horse stretches into the bit and arches the topline muscles.

oxer: A fence with a spread element, usually square (even on both sides) or ascending (back rail is higher than the front).

paces: Various stride lengths within a gait.

phase of suspension: The interval of time in a gait when all four horse's feet are off the ground. The trot and canter have a phase of suspension; the walk does not.

placing pole: Ground pole placed to help teach the horse to take off and land in the correct place.

polo wraps: Cushioned bandage-type wraps that are secured with fabric hook-and-loop fasteners such as Velcro.

rhythm: The even, repeating pattern of footfalls within a gait, such as the one-two-three in the canter. Length of stride remains the same throughout.

shoulder-fore: A two-track movement in which the horse moves with shoulders to one side. Angle is slighter than in the shoulder-in.

shoulder-in: A two-track movement in which the horse moves with shoulders to one side.

side reins: Equipment that attaches from the horse's girth to the bit. Primarily used while lunging to help keep the horse in the right posture, reaching toward the bit.

simple change: Change of lead through the walk or trot.

straightness: Forehand in line with the hindquarters.

stretching circle: Movement judged at lower levels and ridden while schooling. Check to show that the horse has been working on the bit correctly. The horse should remain balanced on the circle while stretching down toward the ground as the rider releases the reins forward.

stride: One cycle of footfalls for each gait.

stride length: Measurement from the beginning of the first footfall to the end of the last footfall. For example, a canter stride length can be twelve feet.

tempo: The rate at which the stride repeats itself. Denotes speed.

ten-meter circle: Circle that is ten meters in circumference. In a standard dressage arena, this circle would touch the centerline.

three-loop serpentine: Three linked twenty-meter circles.

training pyramid/scale: Training sequence in which each new step builds on the last: rhythm, looseness, contact, straightness, impulsion, and collection.

turn-on-the-forehand: Movement that teaches diagonal aid of inside leg to outside rein. Horse steps around the forehand, crossing the hind legs.

turn-on-the-haunches: Movement in which the horse marches around his inside hind leg, which steps in place. Also called walk pirouette.

twenty-meter circle: Circle that is twenty meters in circumference. In a standard dressage arena, this circle would touch the opposite rail.

two-point position: Position in which the third point of contact, the seat, is taken away and the rider's contact on the horse is from the heel up to the knee. The hip angle closes and the seat bones are out of the saddle. Also known as the jumping position.

two-track movement: Movement that requires a horse's body to travel on two different paths.

vertical fence: A straight up-and-down fence.

working gait: Gait that requires very little weight to be carried in the haunches.

Index

Index